Israel in the World

Since independence, Israel has lived with a paradox, needing and seeking legitimacy, understanding, and empathy from the world community while simultaneously discounting the world. This volume reflects upon Israel's troubled attempts to balance its desire to be different from a world that it genuinely needs and that it also wants to be a legitimate member of.

Gathering contributions from distinguished scholars and public figures, this timely book discusses the causes and consequences of Israel's unsettled relations with the world. With essays ranging from an account of Israel's exile mentality and the cosmopolitanism of suffering to a fragmenting international legal order and whether an authentic religious process can transform religion into a powerful lever for peace, the book's innovative analysis will spark both academic and public debate.

Israel in the World: Legitimacy and Exceptionalism will appeal to scholars and students with broad-ranging research interests including Middle East Studies, Israeli Studies and International Relations more generally.

Emanuel Adler is the Andrea and Charles Bronfman Chair of Israeli Studies and Professor of Political Science in the Department of Political Science at the University of Toronto. His publications include: *The Power of Ideology, Security Communities, Communitarian International Relations, Convergence of Civilizations,* and *International Practices.* His current research includes projects on international practices and the evolution of international order and Israel's relations with the world.

Israel in the World

Legitimacy and Exceptionalism

Edited by Emanuel Adler

LONDON AND NEW YORK

First published 2013
by Routledge
2 Park Square, Milton Park, Abingdon, Oxon OX14 4RN

Simultaneously published in the USA and Canada
by Routledge
711 Third Avenue, New York, NY 10017

Routledge is an imprint of the Taylor & Francis Group, an informa business

British Library Cataloguing in Publication Data
A catalogue record for this book is available from the British Library

Library of Congress Cataloging in Publication Data
Israel in the world : legitimacy and exceptionalism / edited by Emanuel
Adler.
p. cm.
Includes bibliographical references and index.
1. National characteristics, Israeli. 2. Israel. 3. Israel——Foreign relations.
4. Israel——Civilization. 5. Arab——Israeli conflict. I. Adler, Emanuel.
DS113.3.I89 2012
327.5694——dc23
2012023256

ISBN: 978-0-415-62415-2 (hbk)
ISBN: 978-0-415-63099-3 (pbk)
ISBN: 978-0-203-08033-7 (ebk)

Typeset in Times
by Taylor & Francis Books

Printed and bound in Great Britain by the MPG Books Group

To Daniel, who I hope will grow up to live in a normal country at peace with the world.

Contents

Notes on Contributors

Emanuel Adler is the Andrea and Charles Bronfman Chair of Israeli Studies and Professor of Political Science in the Department of Political Science at the University of Toronto.

Zvi Bar'el is a member of the *Haaretz* editorial board, a columnist, and the Middle Eastern Affairs analyst of the paper. He is also a lecturer at Sapir Academic College and a senior research fellow at the Center for Iranian Studies at Tel Aviv University.

Michael Barnett is a professor of International Affairs and Political Science at the Elliot School of International Affairs, George Washington University.

Amichai Cohen is the associate dean and a senior lecturer of International Law at the Faculty of Law at Ono Academic College.

Stuart Cohen is a professor of Political Studies and chair of the Academic Council of BESA at the Begin-Sadat Center for Strategic Studies, Bar-Ilan University.

Naomi Chazan is the Dean of the School of Government and Society at the Academic College of Tel Aviv-Yaffo, former president of the New Israel Fund, professor emerita of Political Science (Hebrew University of Jerusalem), and former deputy speaker and Member of the Israeli Knesset.

Michael Melchior is the Chief Rabbi of Norway, the State of Israel's former Minister of Social Affairs and World Jewry, former Deputy Minister of Education and Culture, former Deputy Minister of Foreign Affairs, and an international social activist.

Janice Gross Stein is the Belzberg Professor of Conflict Management and Negotiation in the Department of Political Science and Director of the Munk School of Global Affairs at the University of Toronto.

Michael Walzer is professor emeritus at the School of Social Science, Institute for Advanced Study, Princeton University, and co-editor of *Dissent*.

Acknowledgments

This book originated in a conference of the Association for Israel Studies (AIS) held in Toronto in May 2010 called "Israel in the World," which provided the book's name. Because of the high-quality lectures and papers given at the conference, I recognized that the event's energy and ideas deserved a much broader audience. The conference lectures and papers were reworked into chapters and, together with my introductory chapter, now amount to a tightly structured and systematic volume dealing with the subject of Israel's troubled and ambiguous relations with the world. Surprisingly, because very few books have been published on this topic, *Israel in the World* amounts to an important milestone for understanding Israel among the nations. The book deals with Israel's seemingly paradoxical attempt to balance its desire to be different from a world that it simultaneously genuinely needs and that it also wants to be a legitimate member of. It also helps to place Israel's troubled relationship with the world in perspective by covering a broad spectrum of subjects. They include Israel and the global practice of humanitarianism; Israeli identity; Israeli democracy; Israel in the context of international law and human-rights regimes, religion and peace, asymmetrical conflict, and legitimacy; Israel's ghetto mentality regarding minorities and foreign policy; the relationship between the Israeli–Palestinian conflict and Israel's settlement project, on one hand, and the international community's attitudes toward Israel, on the other; and more. We hope that the book will not only close an existing gap on the subject, but that it will also help spark a research agenda on Israel in the world.

I would like to thank first and foremost Sylvia, my wife, together with whom I organized the AIS conference, and who not only was in large part responsible for its success, but also encouraged me to publish this book every step of the way. My enormous gratitude also goes to Professor Oded Haklai with whom I partnered to put the conference together. He contributed much not only to the conference's fine execution, but also to the substantive ideas behind this book. My thanks also go to Professor Aviva Halamish, who at the time of the conference was president of the Association for Israel Studies. Without her encouragement and guidance, the conference would not have become a success and the book would have not seen the light of day. More generally, I would like to thank the members of the AIS conference's program committee and the AIS board who helped conceive the conference and its subject, and contributed to the conference's accomplishments, thus also making this book possible. In addition, I am also grateful to Professor Janice Stein who encouraged me to pursue the conference and book projects and who provided important substantive advice, as well as to Professors Hindy Nayman and Derek Penslar who partnered with me on financing the conference. I also thank Professors David Cameron, Meric Gertler, and Pekka Sinervo, and two highly perceptive and positively disposed reviewers. I acknowledge the financial support I received from the University of Toronto's Munk School of Global Affairs, the Centre of Jewish Studies, the Faculty of Arts and Science, and the Department of Political Science (all at the University of Toronto), as well as from the Israeli Consulate in Toronto and the American–Israel Cooperative Enterprise. I am also very grateful to Jacqueline Larson for skillfully editing part of the manuscript and preparing it for publication, and to Craig Fowlie, Joe Whiting, Stacey Carter, Mary Tobin, and Kathryn Rylance from Routledge for their guidance and help in putting together this book. Finally, I would like to thank Alena Drieschova, my research assistant, for her extremely useful and competent research assistance.

1 Israel's Unsettled Relations with the World

Causes and Consequences

Emanuel Adler

Can't live with it, can't live without it

Since independence, Israel has lived with a paradox. Israel needs and seeks legitimacy, understanding, and empathy from the world community while simultaneously also discounting the world, which David Ben-Gurion articulated so succinctly with his "Um Shmum."[1] (*Um* represents the acronym in Hebrew for the United Nations (UN) and *shmum* is a dismissive retort.) Discounting the world is also evident in the common Israeli expression "it matters more what Jews do than what the gentiles say." One can find this sentiment's roots in Jewish culture and tradition, for example, the biblical notion that Israel is a people that "shall dwell alone, and shall not be reckoned among the nations." These tension-laden tendencies reflect not only strong cultural dispositions along with issues arising from Israel's troubled birth, development, and existence, but also some of the deep ruptures in Israeli identity: what it means to be Israeli in a globalizing world. "Pushed" by its Jewish past, Israel is shaped by encounters with the Arab "other" and its status as refuge for the Jewish people. But Israeli identity is also "pulled" toward the future by its hunger for modern global economic, cultural, and normative practices, and its desire to be *Or Lagoim* (a light unto other nations). This volume reflects upon Israel's troubled attempts to balance its desire to be different from a world that it genuinely needs and wants to be a legitimate member of.

Israel is without question *in* the world—it needs the world's support and understanding, and in difficult times, when the nation mourns casualties of war and terrorism, it also asks for the world's compassion. For most Israelis, "the world" means primarily the United States, which supports Israel both diplomatically and militarily. Israel's ties with the United States are also special because of the large and powerful Jewish community in America, partly because Israel has culturally become Americanized, and partly because of an affinity of values between the American people and the Israeli people. Israel is also economically and culturally deeply linked to Europe, although the memories of Jewish persecution in Europe (especially of the Holocaust) generate Israelis' uneasiness and suspicion of Europeans. Israel is increasingly plugged into global networks that include emerging powers, such as China and India, and it frequently asks Russia to play a restraining role in the Middle East. When it comes to explaining and promoting its position vis à vis the Arab world, and, in particular, the Palestinians, the whole world is important, country by particular country, including tiny sovereign islands. Jewish communities around the world are a serious concern for Israel, for example, in Latin America, which is why Israel promotes good relations there. In periods of relative quiet, Israel considers even the Middle East to be within the world, but, in times of deep strife, Israel jumps over its immediate neighborhood in order to reach "the outside world," which then seems to start where the Middle East ends.

Because of Israel's economy, which is embedded in global networks, and its industrial, technological, and scientific contributions to the world, Israel has become an important player worldwide. Israel's economy is heavily interdependent with the world via trade, finance, raw materials, and knowledge exchange.[2] One only need consider that Israel is at the top of the Organization of Economic Cooperation and Development (OECD) countries when it comes to venture capital investment as a percentage of GDP,[3] and is second only to the United States with regard to companies listed in NASDAQ. Millions of Israelis travel around the world every year. For example, in 2000, 4.8 million Israelis, or two-thirds of Israel's population at the time, traveled abroad.[4] Israel's thriving art, music, literature, and cinema, which reach the four corners of the earth, and the fact that Israel is related through religion and culture to the origins of Judeo-Christian civilization, make Israel an inseparable part of the global community. For better or worse, there is probably no other country with a population of fewer than eight million people that receives so much media coverage around the world.

Despite all this, Israel deeply mistrusts and discounts the world. Whenever possible, it prefers going it alone. When criticized, Israel tends to fence itself off to protect Israelis from the inhospitable world. In so doing, Israel lives in a "bubble." This "bubble" ideologically and emotionally isolates Israel from the rest of the world and prevents Israelis from reaching out to learn why the world is indeed "against us." From inside their "bubble," Israelis think of themselves as the "chosen people." But they also think that gentile people—who exhibit a false morality and hold pretentious expectations about the "chosen people"—have marked Israel as a source of wrongdoing. This is the world that since antiquity has persecuted and killed Jews, and did everything to contribute to Jews' deep sense of insecurity.

Whether we look at Israel's success in becoming part of global economic networks or at Israel's imposed—some would argue self-imposed—isolation in, and alienation from, the world, the same profound question arises: *why Israel? Why us?* The question of why Israel—a country with fewer than eight million people, without natural resources, and living in a situation of constant security danger—became an important "node" in global economy networks, particularly in high tech, has recently been extensively explored.[5] This book focuses more squarely on Israel's troubled and split relations with the world. From this perspective, the question "why us?" acquires a different meaning:

"why do they always target us?" Why, as Michael Barnett explains in his chapter, has Israel adopted a victimhood identity?

Is Israel's "split personality" a cause of the world's attitudes toward it, or is it a consequence of how the world has treated Jews living among gentiles, and now the state of the Jews? Is it "us" because there is indeed a negative bias toward Israel, lately demonstrated by the Goldstone Report on Israel's human-rights violations in Gaza in 2009? Is it "us" because, as Michael Walzer argues in this book, Israel has still not overcome exile mentality and lacks experience with treating foreign nations and non-Jewish people living in their midst with civic responsibility? Or is it both in that cause becomes consequence and then consequence becomes cause?

One approach to dealing with this question is historical. Although Jews were persecuted and massacred since at least 135 AD, when the Romans killed more than 580,000 Jews and took the rest in captivity to Rome and to an 1800-year-long exile,[6] Israel's relations with the world have still known better days. Before the 1967 Six-Day War, Israel was seen by most in the world with benevolent eyes: as "David" confronting "Goliath," as a new country of an old nation with a new lease on life, which many countries in the world, including most new African countries, wanted to interact with. Perhaps in its early days Israel's support from the world rode on the back of fresh memories of the Holocaust. Perhaps its rather social democratic political ethos and system helped—the kibbutz and Israel's pioneering spirit also promoted a favorable image. And then there were the non-democratic Arab states that vowed to "throw Jews to the sea." Be this as it may, the occupation of Arab territories by Israel as a result of the '67 war, and in particular, the growth of settlements in the occupied territories, helped change Israel's image in the world from "David" to "Goliath," from positive to negative. The more time passed, as settlements became cities and the Palestinians remained hopelessly homeless, the more difficult Israel's position in the world became, to the point that in the last few years not only Israel's behavior, but also its nature as a state of the Jews, has been called into question.

Another approach to dealing with the victim-identity question is by focusing on Israelis' (and Diaspora Jews') deep-seated beliefs about the world. Even if before 1967 most of the world saw Israel in a positive light, to many Israelis the world still "was against us;" let us not forget that Ben-Gurion made his famous remark about "Um Shmum" back in the 1950s.

While they might seem simplistic, two dialectically opposed sets of beliefs account for the dual approach toward the world. On one hand, those who take a pessimist, deterministic, and fatalistic view of Jewish and Israeli history believe that anti-Semitism is the Jews', and more recently Israel's, "other." They thus point to persecution, massacres, and the Holocaust as the high point (or should we call it a low point?) of Jews' deep-seated insecurity (see Barnett in this volume). From this perspective, "the whole world is against us." While liberals around the world self-congratulate about human progress—human rights, humanitarianism, democracy, the rule of law, environmentalism, and the development of a global culture—the world continues to single out Jews, and now Israelis. As a result, Israel should erect high fences, indulge in heightened patriotism, emphasize the uniqueness of the Jewish condition, reject criticism, and follow a defiant path, even at the price of the world's delegitimization.

On the other hand, those who take a more optimistic, non-deterministic, and future-oriented view, while not denying the perverse existence and influence of anti-Semitism, the horrors of the Holocaust, aggression by Israel's enemies, and, more recently, anti-Israeli sentiments around the world, argue nonetheless that nations' attitudes toward Israel are not unrelated to Israel's ambivalent attitude toward the world, and to Israel's behavior toward the Palestinians and Arab minorities within Israel. The argument, in short, is that our condition has become a somewhat self-fulfilling prophecy, but, most important, that it can be changed for the better. Those who suggest this view emphasize that Zionism was all about normalizing the Jewish and, later, Israeli condition, and that only a redefinition of Zionism's main task today as making peace with the Palestinians and the Arab world will enable Israel to become a normal country. According to this view, Israelis must temper their belief that the "world is against us," and their "bunker" or "ghetto"-like practices to radically change their behavior toward the world.

Israel's dual response toward the world can thus partly be traced to the fact that Israel is both a "start-up nation"—which is sometimes euphemistically referred to as "Tel Aviv"—and the ultimate modern "shtetl," sometimes euphemistically referred to as "Jerusalem," where Jews fence themselves from old and new anti-Semites.[7] In this complex *"start-up-shtetl nation,"* "identity is simultaneously universalistic and particularistic, constitutional and tribal."[8] In recent years, however, the balance between universalistic/constitutional forces and particularistic/tribal forces is clearly tilting toward the tribal, heightening Israel's troubles in and with the rest of the world, including the United States.

Israel's troubled relations with the world raise tough questions. Can Israel, or any country, maintain its sovereignty for long without the world's legitimacy? Can Israel survive as a "Jewish and democratic state" by dwelling alone in a world that is increasingly global? Can Israel sustain a nationalist ideology that is out of sync with major normative and institutional trends in the world system, such as humanitarianism, human rights, and the increasing relevance of international law? Is peace a necessary condition for mending Israel's relations with the rest of the world, or will opening Israel to a more constructive dialogue with the world help achieve peace? Is religion part of the problem, or, as Rabbi Michael Melchior argues in this volume, is it also part of the solution to Israel's troubles with the world? All these are relevant questions that subsequent chapters try to provide answers to.

Israel's enemies, detractors, and critics: Why is Israel criticized?

While there does seem to be a special standard the world uses when it comes to Israel, anti-Semitism is only one of many reasons for anti-Israeli attitudes.

Ian Burma, for example, identifies four.[9] First, the use, overuse, and misuse of force by the state of the Jews proves to many, mainly Europeans, that Jews can be aggressors too, thus relieving Europeans from wartime guilt. According to Shaul Arieli, Israel must recognize that by responding to every problem with excessive use of force "it is ignoring the values of the world to which it wants to belong."[10] The "world" is undoubtedly hypocritical when it comes to applying its values to Israel compared to other countries in the world, including the most heinous regimes, let alone the powerful members of the international community. But this point is moot, for what is gained by crying "justice for all" when the reserves of tolerance toward Israel have reached rock bottom and the debate about whether Israel has the right to exist has become normalized even in Western circles favorable to Israel? When it comes to the use of force as a first and final resource, Israel seems to be out of sync with the world; we play into the hand of Israel's detractors. "Israel," reads an editorial in *The Economist,* "is caught in a vicious circle. The more its hawks think the outside world will always hate it, the more it tends to shoot opponents first and ask questions later, and the more it finds that the world is indeed full of enemies."[11] Even worse, according to Zeev Sternhell, "since we ultimately carried out all our wars with the purpose of defeating the Palestinians by perpetuating the situation in the territories, we created the feeling that Israel sees itself existing for the sake of its conquests."[12]

Second, one expects from Israel, a supposedly enlightened Western state, a different type of behavior than one might expect from less or non-modernized peoples. Third, Israel is regarded as a colony of white people, which reminds people of the sins of Western imperialism. Fourth, Israel is a democracy, and, as such, it cannot be judged by the same standards as Assad's Syria.

There are, however, other reasons why Israel is the target of the world's indignation. A fifth reason is that Israel is widely seen, mainly in the Third World, as a proxy for anti-Americanism and for American imperialism in the Middle East. Sixth, the left around the world, which in the past was pre-occupied with revolutions in Latin America and South-African apartheid, more recently adopted the Palestinian cause as its number-one agenda item. Seventh, Arab and Islamic states and non-state actors, and Palestinians, in particular, have skillfully learned to use human-rights organizations around the world to their advantage. This has led to a strategy, as with the 2010 Turkish flotilla affair, to provoke Israel on the assumption that it will respond by using force in front of Al-Jazeera and CNN cameras. It then falls into the trap and gets the rage of world public opinion. As Ariel Levite wrote recently, "having failed to defeat us by force, our remaining enemies have shifted their efforts to trying to weaken the world's support for the justice of our cause and to delegitimize our very existence."[13] Leon Wieseltier echoed this thought when he wrote, after the assault on the *Marmara* in 2010, that "Israel does not need enemies: it has itself."[14] Finally, for socioeconomic reasons, many people in the Middle East region and throughout the Third World cannot stomach the contrast between wealthy Israel, a member of the OECD and a

"Start-Up Nation,"[15] and neighboring states whose combined GNP does not match that of Israel.

None of these reasons is an alternative for a thorough history of the world's—and of specific states'—negative attitudes toward Israel. Such a history, which remains to be written, might clarify whether and who in the world was and is against "us," and whether what lies behind the world's negative attitudes toward Israel is anti-Semitism. Although some studies examine Israel's foreign relations with specific states, such as the United States, France, the UK, and the European Union, it is striking that historiography about Israel and political science analysis, with few exceptions,[16] has neglected analyzing Israel's relations with the world. More study is needed on the background to Israel's attitudes toward the world, which can be traced, for example, to Jewish history, religion, culture, and tradition, the different interpretations of Jewish nationalism, the different and sometimes clashing identities such interpretations helped create, the Yishuv's experience with constituting Israeli identity and institutions, and Israel's interaction with major and lesser powers. It is striking that we lack a sustained analysis of Israel's relations with international institutions, beginning with the UN; with political, economic, and social multilateral global and regional institutions, such as the North Atlantic Treaty Organization, the World Trade Organization, the World Bank, the Council of Europe and the Organization for Security and Cooperation in Europe; with non-governmental institutions (NGOs), such as Amnesty International; and with transnational social movements around the world, such as Greenpeace.

One can only hope that this gap will be filled soon. This introduction can only raise some questions and, particularly, suggest a typology of different groups that oppose Israel. Such a typology may serve to clarify that not all those who criticize Israel are necessarily anti-Semites. It also will serve as a guide to my subsequent analysis of the mechanisms that help explain Israel's, and the world's, mutual sense of estrangement and malaise. It is important to clarify, however, that the following classification is for heuristic purposes only—there exists a great deal of overlap between the different groups, and at times it is difficult to locate the source of antagonism toward Israel in one group or another.

A typology of Israel's detractors

Anti-Semites. The most obvious group of people that stands against Israel is the anti-Semites: those who know they are such, and those whose "best friends are Jews." In the past, and to a lesser extent in the present, anti-Semitism was the main source of Western hatred against Jews. Today, "old style" anti-Semites—whose anti-Semitism can be traced to mostly Christian beliefs against Jews and to socioeconomic circumstances—project their hate not only against individual Jews, which in Western societies is becoming increasingly difficult, but particularly against Israel. "New" anti-Semitism is increasingly associated with Muslims who, for racial and religious reasons, hate Jews and, in particular, Israelis. What unites "old" and "new" anti-Semites, who project their animosity toward the Jewish state, are irrational beliefs that can be traced to emotions, particularly hate, with its background in racial, ethnic, and religious prejudices. Not every Muslim who opposes Israel's existence and the Jewish character of the state is necessarily anti-Semitic. Iran's President M. Ahmadinejad, however, does not hide his anti-Semitism.

Palestinians, Muslims, and more generally the Islamic world. The next category of people who oppose Israel include Palestinians and Muslims in the Middle East and around the world. Palestinians are so far Israel's "other," the enemy, thus their attitudes come directly from their identity, from their grievances, and from their aspirations, at the minimum, for a Palestinian state side by side with Israel, or, at the maximum, for all of Palestine. In polemic academic discussions, Palestinians frequently show keys purporting to belong to a house in Jaffa or Ramle as a symbol of their refugee status and of their dispossession. To the majority of, but not all, Muslims, Israel forcibly removed Palestinians from their land, humiliated Arab states and their armies, and adopted Western ways in the Middle East—Western ways that have no place in the region. With the passage of time, Israel's existence as a state of the Jews became a source of unity among Muslim diversity. That is, opposing Israel became part of Muslim identity from Indonesia to Morocco, not necessarily for religious reasons. Many Muslim politicians, intellectuals, the military, and more generally the masses would like Israel to cease to exist as a Jewish state because Israel is perceived as a cause of Muslim material and cultural neglect and plight. Muslim pride begins with an anti-Israeli position, almost by definition. This is not necessarily anti-Semitism, but an attitude rooted in enmity and conflict for material goods and identity.

Postcolonial liberals. Postcolonial liberals can be identified quite easily on campuses around Europe and North America because of the "keffiyehs" they often symbolically wear around their necks. One can find these people mainly in the West because the roots of their view stem from liberalism, but with a postcolonial twist. To postcolonial liberals, Israel is a colonial entity whose origins go back to the early twentieth century's colonialism in Africa, the Middle East, and Asia. Israelis represent the West. Moreover, they are protected by the United States, which represents modern imperialism. Palestinians, on the other hand, are the indigenous owners of the land—end of discussion. Colonialism has been effectively rooted from the world, thus, Israel is the last case of colonialism in the world. It builds settlements and still colonizes "frontiers" with the "pretenses" that the land was promised to Israel by God, that colonies help spread modern civilization, and that the "natives" have a lot to gain materially from Israel. To postcolonial liberals, therefore, Israel as a Jewish state must be phased out and replaced by a civic-democratic state. Some postcolonial liberals may indeed be anti-Semites, but, for example, many of the students who participate alongside Muslims in "anti-apartheid

Israel week" rallies on campuses across Europe and North America are not necessarily—anti-Semitism actually clashes with their liberal beliefs. Their claim that Israel is an apartheid state, however, confounds Israelis and Diaspora Jews, who, either due to ignorance, or for political instrumental purposes, brand them as anti-Semites.

Kantian liberals. In addition to many other important philosophical works, philosopher Immanuel Kant is well known for the concept of the "categorical imperative,"[17] according to which morality is absolute. In other words, some things are wrong and others are right, period, regardless of whether their consequences bring about opposite effects. Much of the anti-Israeli position one encounters today in Europe, Canada, and to a lesser extent the United States stems from a Kantian liberal perspective. Kantian liberals generally root for Israel as a Jewish and democratic state in secure borders, more or less along the so-called Green Line or 1967 borders (with minor changes). But Kantian liberals cannot morally condone the mistreatment of the Palestinians, and the occupation and settlement of the land where Palestinians are supposed to express their self-determination, just like Israel expresses its own self-determination in its territory within the "Green Line." Kantian liberals are appalled by the settlements, the roadblocks, and the mistreatment of Palestinians by settlers and the Israel Defense Forces (IDF), and cannot understand how turning the Gaza strip into a "Palestinian reserve" is related to Israel's security and well-being. To the contrary, they believe that the siege of Gaza is not only immoral, but also counterproductive to Israel. Yet again, the majority of Israelis and many Jews around the world listen to such criticisms and, even if some of them often express similar views, they automatically place Kantian Liberals within the anti-Semitic camp. Needless to say, Israeli politicians, and Jewish political activists in the Diaspora, mainly from the right, mix moral criticism of Israel with anti-Semitism because, as Avraham Burg cogently put it, "a modicum of anti-Semitism in the West is always sufficient proof of the rightness of the Zionist path as seen through the prism of 'catastrophic Zionism' at its finest."[18] Kantian liberal attitudes cannot be turned around, either by "hasbara," a mixture of justification and propaganda, or by "branding," namely selling Israel's positive image to the world as if it was a bar of soap, but only by changing Israel's practices.

Tough love. This last category refers to Israeli supporters who would like Israel to exist in peace and security. "Tough love" individuals, however, consider Israeli policies to be erroneous and hindering Israel's chances to preserve the Zionist dream. Worried about the harmful effects of both domestic and international Israeli policies, "tough-love" adherents criticize Israeli governments and call on them to change their ways. What differentiates this group from Kantian liberals is mainly the strategic and instrumental calculus of "tough-love" adherents, as opposed to the normative stand of Kantian liberals.

It is difficult to give tough love to Israel and not be seen by Israelis as Israel's detractors. The United States President Barack Obama belongs to this category. If only for reasons of national interest and domestic politics, Obama would like Israel to continue to exist within recognized borders and to live in peace with security. He thus cannot understand how and why Netanyahu's rightist coalition government follows policies that in Obama's view diminish Israel's security, delegitimize Israel in the eyes of the world, make it more difficult for the United States to support Israel (e.g., against Iran's nuclear ambitions), empower the Palestinians in world forums, and may one day lead Israel to become, *by default,* either an apartheid state, or a "state of all its citizens." Some Israelis and American Jews, however, wrongly believe that Obama is not only a Muslim, whose middle name is Hussein, but also an anti-Semite.

There are plenty of well-meaning "tough love" people in Europe, other countries in the Western world, and even in Third World countries. By branding every gentile who dares to criticize Israel as an anti-Semite, however, Israeli politicians and public opinion, as well as many Diaspora Jews, are in danger of making their prophecy self-fulfilling. It is particularly difficult for a Diaspora Jew to give Israel "tough love." The fact that Jews need to demonstrate that their criticism of Israel comes out of love for Israel shows the difficulty they encounter in legitimately criticizing Israel without being branded as anti- or post-Zionist, or, worse, as self-hating Jews. Israel's current government strategy to deal with "tough love" is to define any position that criticizes government policies, in particular settlement policies, as anti-patriotic, anti-Zionist, and anti-Israeli.

Israel's attitudes toward an "antagonistic" world

When considering the complexity and variety of negative attitudes toward Israel, it is hard to believe how detached Israel is from how it is perceived by the world. To most Israelis, the whole world is against it. According to Ephraim Yaar and Tamar Hermann's August 2010 Peace Index,[19] 56 percent of the Jewish public in Israel believed that "the whole world is against us." Moreover, a large majority of Israeli Jews (a whopping 77 percent) believe that it makes no difference what Israel does or how far it may go on the Palestinian issue: the world will continue to be critical of Israel. Furthermore, 54 percent of Israeli Jews believe that Israel is completely isolated and, moreover, 48 percent of Israel's Jewish population considers that it should not take world public opinion into account. When it comes to the United States, 71 percent of Jewish respondents argued that Israel should take Washington's positions into account. To most Israelis, the US *is* the world—everything else is negligible, dispensable, or the subject of instrumental manipulation. These findings are important because, first, they show that most Israelis, at least in recent times, adopt the fatalistic view of Israel's relations with the world. Second and related, they suggest that, even if 42 percent of Israel's Jewish population disagree with the notion that all the world is against us, "many of the same individuals believe that Israel's actions and policies are not the main source of the criticism directed at the Jewish state."[20]

This means that most Israelis believe that the Jewish condition is to be hated by the world, most likely due to anti-Semitism, perhaps also due to religious reasons. In the past it was the crusaders. Then it was Hitler. Today it is the Muslim world and increasingly the rest of the world. Everything our enemies, and their supporters around the world, do actually proves Israelis right. Israelis retreat from occupied territories, for example, from Lebanon in 2000, and from the Gaza Strip in 2005, and what do Israelis get in return but increased threats and attacks? Although it's sustained by only a small number of people in Israel, the alternative view is that Israel's actions are not unrelated to negative attitudes against it. Israeli Arabs' attitudes are the reverse of the majority of the Jewish population in Israel: "a large majority (75%) disagrees with the maxim that the whole world is against Israel, and a majority of 54% sees a connection between Israel's actions and world criticism."[21] But 33 percent of the Israeli Jewish population also shares this "Arab" view. To quote Ariel Levite, an Israeli whose security credentials cannot be questioned:

> Again and again, we make our few friends left sick of us, and over and over we push the skeptics and neutrals into the arms of our inveterate hate-driven foes. We contribute to this not only by balking at peace, continuing "illegal" (as we call it) settlement, wanton misconduct in the territories, and barring intellectuals from entering Israel. We are also callous toward the many Arab citizens who wish to continue living with us in peace as Israelis.[22]

This raises the fundamental question I referred to earlier, whether criticism or, worse, hate of Israel is detached from Israel's actions, or whether it is related as cause, or as a chain of circular causes and consequences of Israel's own actions. The same question has been asked before regarding hate toward Jews throughout history: is it the world, is it us, or is it both? In the following pages, I attempt to show that there are several mechanisms that bind Jews/ Israel and its detractors and haters in a vicious circle of causes and consequences, which so far have been difficult if not impossible to break. While alluding here and there to the Jewish condition among other nations before the State of Israel, I suggest three such mechanisms at work when it comes to Israel and its detractors: 1) a socio-psychological mechanism, 2) nationalism and its excesses, and 3) intellectual or moral failure, or both. While the socio-psychological mechanism and nationalism partly explains the situation, the "double-bind failure" is a necessary condition for why Israel did not become a normal country among nations and does not "dwell in the world."

Of causes and consequences: Israel, the world, and the abyss

On 31 January 1961, Yaacov Herzog, then Israel's ambassador to Canada, and Professor Arnold Toynbee, British historian, met to debate Israel. The debate was triggered by comments Toynbee made days before to the effect that what Israel did to the Palestinians in the War of Independence (1947–8) was similar to what the Nazis did to the Jews. Furthermore, Toynbee argued that Israel had become a "fossilized civilization." At the debate, which even Toynbee's wife admitted Ambassador Herzog won,[23] Herzog asked the crucial question "Why do you choose us?" Why, if as Toynbee admitted there were also Arab massacres, had he singled out Israel? "Why didn't you write that Britain and almost every other country in the world falls under this definition?" With such a line of questioning, Herzog led Toynbee to admit that Israel was not different from other nations in the world.[24] Ambassador Herzog also forced Toynbee to admit that Israel had been de-fossilized, although Toynbee argued that ultra-nationalism was still the danger.[25]

The perennial question "Why us?" raises my main question: is Israel's troubled relationship with the world a cause, a consequence, or both? In Arnold Toynbee's case, his anti-Israeli views stem from deep Christian religion-driven anti-Semitism. As we saw, however, animosity toward Israel also emanates from groups of people who are not anti-Semites, and whose views are colored by what Israel is, or rather is becoming, and by its behavior, particularly toward the Palestinians and Arab citizens of Israel.

Although I said I would address these questions by identifying three non-mutually exclusive hypotheses that link causes and consequences, it is important to clarify that the following pages are not about justice, values, or policy. In other words, I am not seeking to determine who is right. Moreover, by no means do I argue that Jews may be responsible for anti-Semitism, hate against Jews and, more recently, against Israel. Rather, I seek to identify the root mechanisms of Israel's insecurity and sense that "the whole world is against us," and, therefore, that "we shall dwell alone, and shall not be reckoned among the nations." It is also important to emphasize that these hypotheses only scratch the subject's surface. A full analysis of the Jewish condition, and recently of Israel versus the world would require volumes going back to Jewish antiquity, analyzing Jewish religion, anti-Semitism, Spain's "Golden Age," and Jewish emancipation.

One answer to the question "Why us?" and what causes what—both in Jewish history, and in Israel's contemporary context—is *the world*. I should know—all my family was killed in the Holocaust, except my parents; my mother barely survived in an underground hole for two years, thanks to a "righteous gentile" who saved her life. According to this view, it always was the world: anti-Semitism (old and new), persecution, crusades, pogroms, the Holocaust (in which six million Jews were brutally murdered), then Arabs fighting Jews since the beginning of the twentieth century, and now Ahmadinejad's Iran, Hezbollah, and Hamas. Obviously, not the whole world is against us. There were and are "righteous gentiles," but this does not change the fact that throughout history Jews have had to endure persecution and extermination. Few recent studies express more vividly this understanding than the United Nations' "Goldstone Report" (see also Janice Stein's chapter in this volume), which, investigating human-rights atrocities allegedly committed by Israel during the 2009 "Cast Lead" operation in the Gaza Strip, scarcely subjected Hamas to strong criticism for throwing 10,000 missiles against southern Israel throughout the 1990s, but did indict Israel for purposely committing the atrocities in Gaza. Although Judge Goldstone, a Jew who self-identified as "Zionist," retracted his views as they came across in the Report, the UN Report stands and is unlikely to be revised.

The other answer is: "*it is us.*" As Bradley Burston wrote,

> The right is terrified of peace. And in the end, the right's fear of peace will be the death of Israel ... They are afraid of peace because they are afraid of the world. They dismiss fellow Jews who want to see a two-state solution—a majority of Israelis—as unrealistic, as living in a bubble. The name of the bubble these moderates live in, however, is planet earth. The right, meanwhile, wants to wall off Israel as the world's last remaining legally mandated Jewish ghetto ... A place which, if suffocating and insufferable, still seems safer than the scary world outside ... I have come to envy the people who hate Israel, because they cannot feel the tragedy in the phenomenal possibility, the depth and breadth of humanity that is going to waste here.[26]

Of course the people of Israel elected the right to power and there are very good historical and contemporary reasons to distrust the world. Moreover, it is not just "the right," but also the entire mainstream political system, including the Labor Party, which has taken a skeptical position about the world, as illustrated by Ben-Gurion's (Labor) "Um Shmum."

But this does not matter, retorts Burton, and everybody who shares his views: Israel is becoming a recluse state and in the end our fear of the world will doom us. This is especially because Israel has only three alternatives when it comes to the Palestinians: 1) a viable two-state solution now, because this alternative may fade away soon, 2) an apartheid state, de facto a Jewish state between the Mediterranean sea and the Jordan river, which means the moral and probably also the material end of Israel later on, and 3) a "state of all of its citizens," de facto, one Palestinian state in the same area.

Hypotheses one: "The abyss"

This hypothesis is heuristically related to the oft-repeated famous Aphorism 146 from Friedrich Nietzsche's *Beyond Good and Evil:* "He who fights with monsters should look to it that he himself does not become a monster. And when you gaze long into an abyss the abyss also gazes into you."[27] The causal chain this hypothesis refers to is psychological and sociological. Throughout history, the world has been a monster for the people of Israel, so, when the people of Israel finally achieved their state, the monster showed its face again, this time in the image of the "Muslim other." Because Israeli Jews now see monsters everywhere in the world, they therefore perceive themselves as constantly facing an abyss and, in the process, have come to imitate and resemble the monsters they have projected everywhere as threatening a new abyss.

This explanation combines affect—mainly fear and insecurity, and especially, but not exclusively, on the political right, self-pride—and domestic politics, particularly, Israeli government officials' need to show they are patriots, more Zionist than their political rivals, always ready to consider any alternative, including the use of force, to protect Israelis and, by extension, the Jewish people as a whole. This way, Israelis turn themselves into monsters in the eyes of the world; they are incapable of making peace given their own so-called realism and belief that the world understands and operates only by force.

This mechanism is also fueled by a Jewish legacy of never being able to be part of a larger community, because, as Martin Buber argues, doing so would go against Jewish people's unique identity and their special bond with God. The result is a people who cannot define itself as part of the larger community— this feeds the monster![28] Israel is repeating the same pattern; it is not defining itself as other nations do, but rather is acting according to its own interpretation of international law, and taking the international community into account only when it serves the Jewish interest. "Um Shmum" refers back to Israel's "realism," which, according to Israelis, all other nations abide by. These attitudes, and the overlying cynicism that goes with them, also feed the monster! Having to fight the monster, pushed from the past by a sense that Israelis cannot be part of the larger community, in this case, the community of humankind, engulfed by feelings of insecurity and fear, and moved by politics and identity, Israelis gaze into the abyss and become monsters themselves in the eyes of the world—the abyss gazes back at Israel. While this hypothesis is by no means related to how Nietzsche himself understood the Jews or what Jews should do about their own condition, I do try to avoid the most stereotypical interpretations of Nietzsche's Aphorism 146, for example, that if you look at evil long enough it will become a part of you.[29]

Hypothesis two: Nationalism, the solution that became the problem

This hypothesis argues that basic insecurity, which has driven Jewish existence at least since 135 AD, found its solution in Jewish nationalism or Zionism, starting in the mid-1800s. Zionism encouraged Jews to come to Palestine in waves of ascendance (Aliyah) to settle the land of Israel. The more Zionists arrived in Zion, the more threatened Arabs became, so it did not take long for cycles of violence to begin—and they have continued ever since. This violent reaction by the local Arabs, and by neighboring Arab states, in addition to the hostility of the Muslim world, and the increasing negative reaction to Israel's use of force against other peoples, particularly since 1967, helped turn Jewish nationalism, which was the solution for the plight of the homeless Jewish people, into Israel's problematic relationship with the world. Nationalism, which became particularly imbued with strong ethnic and religious connotations since 1977, when the Likud came into power and de facto replaced Labor's long-held hegemony, turned into what Martin Buber called "arbitrary nationalism." According to Buber's 1921 interpretation of nationalism,

> We hoped to save Jewish nationalism from the error of making an idol of the people. We have not succeeded. Jewish nationalism is largely concerned with being "like unto all the nations," with affirming itself in the face of the world without affirming the world's reciprocal power ... The nationalistic crisis in Judaism is in sharp, perhaps too sharp, relief in the pattern of the nationalistic crises of current world history. In our case, more clearly than in any other, the decision between life and death has assumed the form of deciding between legitimate and arbitrary nationalism.[30]

Arbitrary nationalism, which increasingly became ethnic based, and was fed by messianic currents initiated a century ago by Rabbi Avraham Isaac Kook, led to the settlement project as a legitimate Zionist endeavor. According to later interpretations of Rabbi Kook's political theology, settling the entire land of Israel would not only help bring about religious redemption, but also redemption from insecurity, which Jews experienced through the ages. Delegitimization of Israel by the world followed, which led Israel to feel that the world is against us—and, in fact, led to ongoing insecurity.

This hypothesis first finds a causal link between Jewish insecurity, or the search for security, and nationalism. According to Buber, not wanting to be classified, Jews' inability to fit into the larger community gave meaning to Israel's uniqueness, which led to the solution of being classified as a nation. Nationalism and the Jewish nation would provide badly needed security to the Jewish people. But when nationalism becomes "arbitrary" and is taken to ethnic and religious extremes, it leads to deception and self-righteousness, and to the screening of information that does not fit with self-images of the authentic ethnic nation, and/or religious beliefs of redemption. If only "we" hold to the "liberated" territories and settle the land of Israel's frontiers—a practice that, like the American move westward, passed from the face of the earth long ago—Israel will be redeemed, both from religious and security perspectives.

Enter the other causal link: the more Israel's core Zionist beliefs and practices are based on "arbitrary nationalism," the stronger the response from the community of nations and the delegitimization of Israel, the more official Israel, under pressure, responds with a combination of a self-destructive sense of self-righteousness and victimhood, on one hand, and pride and a resort to force, on the other hand. These excesses lead obviously to counter-reactions, and counter-reactions lead to counter-counter-reactions and to the feeling that "we shall dwell alone, and shall not be reckoned among the nations."

The way out of the vicious circle would be to regain legitimacy and the world's understanding by going forward with a historic and just settlement with the Palestinians. But what else is new? In an address to the Twelfth Zionist Congress in 1921, Buber said that:

Either a healthy reaction will set in that will overcome the danger heralded by nationalism, and also nationalism itself, which has now fulfilled its purpose; or nationalism will establish itself as the permanent principle, in other words, it will exceed its function, press beyond its proper bounds and—with overemphasized consciousness—displace the spontaneous life of the nation. Unless some force arises to oppose this process, it may well be the beginning of the downfall of the people.[31]

This argument can be countered with the claim that there is nothing arbitrary and illegitimate with ethnic and religious nationalism. After all, it is the Jewish people who came to build the third commonwealth in the Land of Israel. Moreover, even if nationalism may lead to excesses, the blame is on the other side—the side that wants to finish Israel up with missiles, nuclear weapons, or through merely demographic trends. But, as I said before, causal relations are not about who is right or just, and this argument that the other side is to blame begs the question because it does not address the insidious social trap that arbitrary nationalism poses to the nation. Either God will once more help Israel "flee Egypt" and make it free, or Israel will continue to be embattled forever in the tragic belief that time means surviving a week at a time, or, worse, that time is in Israel's favor.

Also tragic, if we follow the idea of nationalism as a problematic solution, is the notion that the fruits of Israel as a "start-up nation," and the part of our identity that lives "in the world" may be wasted and depleted. As Bernard Avishai remarked, Israel is "Singapore" when it comes to its economy and "Serbia" when it comes to its ideology and political practices.[32] Israel, in fact, is a nation with a richer and longer pedigree than Serbia. If, however, as Buber argued in 1921, Israelis do not legitimize their national enterprise as being about national self-determination, rather than building "fortress Israel," or, worse, the third temple, then the world may one day turn against Israel as it did against Serbia. This brings us directly to hypothesis number three.

Hypothesis three: Intellectual and/or moral failure

According to this hypothesis, Israel's relations with the world result from either moral and/or intellectual failure. If Israelis know that, by continuing with the settlement process, Palestinians have real difficulty going forward with the peace process and Israelis nevertheless do nothing to stop the settlements, thus bringing upon Israel the world's rage, this amounts to moral failure. If Israeli leaders understand that sovereignty cannot be determined only internally, but must be externally legitimized—if they know what the price is in terms of relations with Europe, the developing world, and perhaps one day the United States and the American Jewish community[33]—but, due to ideology, domestic political considerations, and emotional factors, they do not change course and do not take the necessary political steps to arrive at a compromise with the Palestinians, this is also moral failure.

If, however, Israeli leaders really do not understand, or are too busy navel gazing to understand all these issues, and the people of Israel are too tired, absent-minded, or plainly scared to change course before the "Titanic hits the iceberg," this is intellectual failure. If Israelis do not understand that, as long as the settlement process continues, it will be impossible for Palestinian leaders to give up their anti-Israeli identity, then this represents intellectual failure, and condemns Israel to be isolated, ostracized, and delegitimized.

No matter how you look at it, Israeli leaders, and the Israeli masses in their passivity, may thus be guilty of intellectual failure, moral failure, or both. This hypothesis is compounded by the notion that avoiding intellectual or moral failure requires that Israel become a normal country. Becoming a normal country, however, requires making peace fast, before the window of opportunity for a viable two-state solution closes up and Israel remains with only the one-state alternative, either the "state of all of its citizens," which Palestinians and some Israeli Arabs would like, or the greater Israel alternative, which Israelis on the right can only dream about. To change the situation drastically involves a change in identity. In other words, Zionism must be redefined from settling a frontier to making peace with the neighborhood and the world in order to save Zionism and the state of the Jews. This change could occur through either learning or catastrophe. The end of the Cold War and of South African Apartheid and the victories of the civil rights movement in America are examples of cases in which identity change came about by learning. Normative change took place and people began thinking outside the box—they dramatically redefined the problem they confronted, and then they found a solution through learning and peaceful means. By contrast, Germany, Japan, and to some extent France during the Second World War changed their identities, practices, and behavior and thereby their relations with the rest of the world only after a catastrophe hit them hard. I want Israel to change, make peace with its neighbors, become a normal country, and dwell in the world via learning rather than catastrophe.

To join the global community, change the meaning of Zionism

The solution to the Jewish and Israeli perennial problem of insecurity, and to Israel's inability to fit within the world as a normal country—a country that attracts immigration less because of its military heroic actions than because of its thriving cultural life and economic dynamism—lies in redefining the meaning of Zionism.

Zionism developed in the nineteenth century, when empires ruled the world, when the world was divided between "civilized" nations and lands inhabited by "natives," when colonialism was taken as natural, when there were no global human rights that competed with sovereignty as the constitutive principle of the inter-state system, when wars were the natural way of settling political problems, and when international communication meant sending a telegram. Gone are the days in which a country could dwell alone in the world and fence itself off from the world. The world today does not mean only two hundred-odd states, materially speaking, but also a structure made up of social, economic, cultural, and political-legal networks that reach almost every household on earth.

Moreover, neither power nor war is what they were in the past. Back then, the stronger side won and imposed its will on the weaker side. Today, as Janice Stein's chapter shows, asymmetrical warfare has replaced war in the trenches; the weak, a bunch of badly armed unsophisticated terrorists, can destroy a city, deter a much militarily stronger power, and use the structure of human rights in the world to provoke the strong side to respond, thus bringing the world's rage against it. Think about the world as a giant audience that watches actors perform in a global scene. Act one: Hezbollah kidnaps several Israeli soldiers; act two: Israel destroys half of Beirut; act three: after 40 days of warfare and its photographs transmitted through Facebook and Twitter around the world, the play comes to an end and the audience retires to decide who won. Israeli officers may be proud that the play ended with much of Israel's deterrence capability restored, but the audience voted and Hezbollah won. It is quite obvious, and, if it is not, it should be, that power is much more diffuse now. The United States and the North Atlantic Treaty Organization combined, let alone Israel, cannot impose their will on other nations, or even on relatively small, armed groups, without paying an impossible domestic and international price.

Most important for our purposes, the meaning of security and insecurity has changed. Israel came to the Land of Israel to fence itself off from enemies, anti-Semites, and persecutors. It built the strongest army in the Middle East and one of the strongest armies in the world. Unfortunately, there are objectively few places where Jews are still as insecure as in Israel today. Security in a global world cannot emanate from the power of the gun only. Obviously, Israel should keep its defenses up, for it is still surrounded by enemies that wish its destruction. Security, however, emanates primarily from coming to terms with the world—from interconnectedness, understanding the world, being one step ahead, and legitimacy in the eyes of other nations.

While Zionism (and its diverse movements) changed its territorial ambitions, notions of collective mission, and relations to the Jewish Diaspora during the last century,[34] Zionism's deep constitutive collective understanding, in contrast, for example, to postwar European nationalism, did not evolve.[35] Zionism's fundamental conceptions, such as ethnic-based exceptionalism, abnormality as a "normal" state, and acting in response to anti-Semitism, are at odds with many changes in the world, such as globalization, human-rights movements, global humanitarian norms, and normative changes regarding the use of force. While Israel must keep its guard high against anti-Semitism, security for the Jewish people, and mainly for Israel, will come only from adapting to the times and to a changing world. One hundred years ago, pioneering and patriotism may have meant the few standing alone against "primitive" marauders, but, in this day and age, Zionism can no longer mean settling a frontier. Fulfilling and securing the goal of Jewish self-determination, Zionism needs to put its historic feud with the Palestinians behind it once and for all, dividing the land, as A. B. Yehoshua says "every stone and every part of it,"[36] and changing its identity.

To achieve real security, Israel needs more diplomacy and less use of force: it needs to be wise rather than right, and to drastically change the nature of its relations with the region. All this is particularly urgent after the "Arab Spring," which is transforming the entire region, while Israel only gazes in disbelief. True, there is no more anarchic region in the world than the Middle East, so the best Israel can do is, as Ronald Reagan used to say, "trust but verify." But realism can take us only so far; its prophecies tend to become self-fulfilling. In other words, insecurity breeds insecurity and the result will be living by the sword forever, hoping to survive the next week, month, and year, and always with personal and state insecurity.

Perhaps Israelis would feel more secure after dividing the land with the Palestinians if regional security and economic regimes and institutions were developed, though these regimes would not solve Israel's insecurity stemming from Iran's nuclear weapons. However, if Iran is not peacefully or forcefully dissuaded from developing nuclear weapons, Israel still has the capability to deter them. Regional peace could also help defuse much of the regional animosity that makes it easier for Iran to provoke and fight Israel. Moreover, regional security regimes could provide Israel not only with a sense of self, but also with a sense of place. For instance, Israel would feel more secure were a Mediterranean identity and institutions developed, a Mediterranean Union of sorts, not as a device for supporting French policy in the region, but for changing dramatically the nature of the region.

Treating neighbors that wish to extend a hand with dignity and respect, regardless of their religion, ethnic background, and color of skin, and applying the golden rule to Israeli minorities, namely treating them as Jews would wish to be treated in foreign lands, would provide security because security in today's world depends not only on the barrel of the gun, but also on the accumulation of symbolic capital and legitimacy, which can be spent when circumstances require. Sustaining not only Jewish but also a democratic culture in Israel would secure Israel because, these days, despots might still stick to their guns and avoid going to the trash of history for a little while longer, but only democracies can get the respect of most nations and international institutions.

Skeptics will say that, as long as Israel is surrounded by enemies that wish to destroy it, and insofar as the world is and always was against "us," these points are merely idealistic dreaming. What skeptics do not realize, however, is that in saying so, and *doing as they say*, they activate and reactivate the vicious circle of causes and consequences I described earlier. Rather than responding passively to a world that is tired of Israel's occupation of the West Bank and of wars in the Middle East, and that wants to solve other pressing problems in the Middle East, such as those related to the "Arab Spring," a bold Israeli initiative is needed that can revolutionize the Middle East, as much if not more than the Arab revolutions. Security is achieved by outsmarting the opponent, being one step ahead, and taking active measures that are least expected, rather than passively reacting to what others do because of fear that taking the initiative would upset the status quo and, moreover, "God forbid," undermine a government's coalition.

Bradley Burston is right: Israel is afraid of peace because it is afraid of the world and it always has been. Therefore, the time has come to break with the vicious circle of causes and consequences—to normalize Israel, and, by extension, the Jewish condition, by gaining symbolic capital and legitimacy with a world to which Israel belongs, though Israel has been reticent to admit it. This will help adapt Zionism to the twenty-first century, bring Israelis closer to enjoying peace, even if, at the same time, more than most other nations of the world, Israel will need to keep defenses up for when they are really needed. Once we will be *in* the world, at least part of the world will be within us, and thus also "with us."

Plan of the book

To analyze some of the subjects I've raised here, our book brings together seven leading scholars and/or practitioners. In chapter two, Michael Walzer argues that Israel has not yet overcome "exile" mentality, according to which Jews never had to deal with ruling over others, fighting wars (and criticizing the fighting), and handling foreign policy, particularly forging alliances in the society of states. Israel thus lacks "civic responsibility," which in Walzer's view is what David Ben-Gurion meant by the Hebrew word *mamlachtiyut*. Too many Israelis live in their new state as if they were still in exile. This is especially so among religious Jews, but the carryover of exilic attitudes also affects secularists. Overcoming this situation will require learning from the wisdom of foreigners and speaking to one another. Jews, says Walzer, have to learn what it means to be sovereign and how sovereignty is best enacted.

In chapter three, Michael Barnett argues that Israel's increasing lack of legitimacy and sense of victimhood can be traced back to a growing gap between a cosmopolitanism of suffering and an Israel that increasingly presents itself as being a "people apart." This argument relies on four lines of reasoning. First, the world has become increasingly cosmopolitan to the point that a cosmopolitanism of suffering became the defining expression of our identification with distant others. Second, a cosmopolitanism of suffering initially favored the Jews and Israel but it no longer does. Third, while Judaism and Jewish history are a changing composite of particularism and universalism, Israel has increasingly answered the "Jewish Question"—whether and how Jews should maintain their identity in the world—by relying on nationalist and religious particularism. Consequently, while Israel arguably sees itself as a victim, the rest of the world increasingly struggles to identify with Israeli suffering. Finally, Israel's sense of being a "people apart" might be both a cause and effect of its sense of victimization.

In chapter four, Amichai Cohen and Stuart Cohen argue that throughout its history Israel has shown itself to be sensitive to international law requirements. Over time, however, changes have occurred in the mindset within which that attitude is framed. Broadly speaking, during the early years of statehood, Israel's expressions of respect for international law articulated an essentially *utilitarian* attempt to gain legitimacy. More recent pronouncements, by contrast, reflect two other developments, which to some extent interact. One is the growing diffusion of the decision-making process in Israel regarding national-security affairs. The second is the growing influence within Israeli political and public life of several institutions, governmental and non-governmental, whose respect for international law is based on their perception of the intrinsic legitimacy of that corpus. The chapter illustrates the impact of those processes, *inter alia*, through an examination of the influence exerted by the IDF's International Law Branch (DABLA), especially with reference to targeted killings.

In chapter five, Naomi Chazan argues that, at precisely the same time that democratically driven upheavals are spreading throughout the Arab world, Israel is in a process of de-democratization, not only dividing Israelis, but also increasingly splitting the Jewish world. The question of Israel's place in the world has been internalized; the enemy from outside is now being hunted at home. The civic nature of Israeli identity, as defined by its founders, is being questioned by a growing neo-nationalist surge bent on replacing the universal and Jewish values of equality, justice, and tolerance with an ethnically driven mindset that ties the connection between the land and the people to an exclusivist agenda that denies diversity and denigrates pluralism. The chapter traces several recent campaigns against critical voices in order to understand why this process is taking place, and what are its dynamics, methods, effects, and responses. Chazan contends that systematic efforts to delegitimize and ultimately destroy alternative groups and viewpoints in Israel are contributing directly to undermining the foundations of Israel's democracy and, by extension, the basis for its international legitimacy. The erosion of Israel's commitment to democracy weakens its internal fabric as well as its international viability. From this perspective, the determination of Israel's own identity lies, first and foremost, in its own hands.

In chapter six, Janice Stein argues that Israel's conduct in war stands at the exposed shard of a fragmenting international legal order. Brought to attention recently by the Goldstone Report, Israel's conduct in an "asymmetrical war" raises all the contradictions of a legal order that is fragmenting, evolving, and yet, as flawed and incomplete as it is, critical to the legitimation of power and the use of force. According to Stein, asymmetrical war's defining characteristic is a contest for legitimacy, whereas the front is everywhere and the battlefield is among civilians, in neighborhoods, in streets, in cafés. It is this kind of "asymmetrical war" that Israel has fought for the last two decades, on one front or another, within a legal framework fraught with contradiction and ambiguity. That legal framework was constructed within a framework of a war between states, between armies, in a defined battle space, which is now increasingly rare. The question for Israel, and for others who fight asymmetrical wars, is what constitutes a legal and just response; the two are not always the same. Unfortunately, says Stein, the Goldstone Report ignored all these complexities and contradictions and missed the chance to push forward the discussion of international law in a radically changed context. In this sense, Israel represents one shard of a fragmented legal order. In its wars, it exposes the inadequacies of the existing global corpus of the laws of war, a body of law developed for wars no longer fought and silent on many of the issues in the wars that are fought.

Chapter seven, by Zvi Bar'el, looks at Israel's problematic relationship with the world from the perspective of the Israeli–Palestinian conflict and the struggle for Israeli identity. While the Middle East is embroiled in democratic revolutions, Israel, which seems immune to international pressure to solve its conflict with the Palestinians, is crystallizing its identity as a Jewish state—an identity that builds on dictates imposed on it by the *inner-Diaspora*, the settlers, who in the course of forty years made Israel their satellite state. The State of Israel, thus, is engaged in a national struggle with the settler state. Furthermore, the raison d'être of Israel has become to protect the settlements' existence. The *mother-state* became a servant state. Palestinians have the same problem. They too have two states, one in Gaza and one in the West Bank and East Jerusalem. They too have no final borders, yet, like Israelis, they are in search of the territory that will define their nation. Hamas behaves like the settlers; both want their Motherland (Israel and the Palestinian authority, respectively) to adopt their ideology; both consider their primary state to be a menace to the national vision; and neither wants to detach completely from their primary state. Moreover, both prefer the four-state situation to the two-state solution. The corollary is clear: Israel and the Palestinians are locked in internal negotiations with their enclaves and not with each other. The only way out depends on Israel considering the settlements as a debatable territory, imposing its identity on the settlers, and recognizing that there is one Palestinian people rather than two. Palestinians, on the other hand, must recognize Israel's limits of power in dealing with the settlements.

In the final chapter, Rabbi Michael Melchior presents religion as a guiding force in human life, history and conflict, and, by extension, the Israeli–Palestinian conflict. He argues that, despite the religious overtones of war and conflict throughout history, those involved on the ground and in peacemaking processes consciously ignore these elements. Instead, we have made the mistake of imposing Western liberal values, and the separation of church and state in particular, onto conflict in a region where politics and religion are inextricably entwined. Therefore, in order to bring peace to Israel and the Middle East, we must adopt a new approach to conflict resolution that merges commitment to religion with the values of human life and democracy.

Notes

1 Cabinet Debate, 29 March 1955.
2 Dan Senor and Saul Singer, *Start-Up Nation: The Story of Israel's Economic Miracle*, New York: Twelve, 2009, pp. 11–13.

3 Guy Grimland, "OECD Report Finds Israel as Top Country for Venture Capital", *Haaretz*, 3 July 2011 <http://www.haaretz.com/business/oecd-report-finds-israel-as-top-country-for-venture-capital-investment-1.370957>.
4 Uri Ram, *The Globalization of Israel: McWorld in Tel Aviv, Jihad in Jerusalem*, London: Routledge, 2008, p. 66.
5 Ram, *The Globalization of Israel*; Senor and Singer, *Start-Up Nation*.
6 "Bar Kokhba," *Encyclopedia Judaica*, Jerusalem: Veler. See also Yehoshafat Harkabi, *The Bar-Kokhba Syndrome: Risk and Realism in International Relations*, New York: Rossel Books, 1982.
7 Ram, *The Globalization of Israel*; Yaron Ezrahi, *Rubber Bullets: Power and Conscience in Modern Israel*, Berkeley: University of California Press, 1997; Emanuel Adler, *Communitarian International Relations: The Epistemic Foundations of International Relations*, London: Routledge, 2005, pp. 243–58.
8 Ram, *The Globalization of Israel*, p. 208.
9 Ian Burma, "Is Israel a Normal Country?" *Haaretz*, 9 July 2010 <http://www.haaretz.com/print-edition/opinion/is-israel-a-normal-country-1.300934>.
10 Shaul Arieli, "The Fixation of Power," *Haaretz*, 27 October 2010 <http://www.haaretz.com/print-edition/opinion/the-fixation-of-power-1.298498>.
11 "Israel Siege Mentality," *The Economist*, 3 June 2010 <http://www.economist.com/node/16274081?story_id=E1_TGNSQDRT>.
12 Zeev Sternhell, "Time to Pay the Bill," *Haaretz*, 11 June 2010 <http://www.haaretz.com/print-edition/opinion/time-to-pay-the-bill-1.295528>.
13 Ariel Levite, "It's Not the PR, Stupid," *Haaretz*, 8 June 2010 <http://www.haaretz.com/print-edition/opinion/it-s-not-the-pr-stupid-1.294831>.
14 Leon Wieseltier, "Operation Make the Whole World Hate Us," *The New Republic*, 3 June 2010 <http://www.tnr.com/article/politics/75287/operation-make-the-world-hate-us>.
15 Senor and Singer, *Start-Up Nation*.
16 See, for example, Michael Brecher, *Decisions in Israel's Foreign Policy*, New York: Oxford University Press, 1974; Alan Dowty, "Israel's Foreign Policy and the Jewish Question," *International Affairs*, vol. 3, no. 1, March 1999; Uri Bialer, *Between East and West: Israel's Foreign Policy*, Cambridge: Cambridge University Press, 1990; Sasson Sofer, *Zionism and the Foundations of Israeli Diplomacy*, Cambridge: Cambridge University Press, 2007; Alexander Yakobson and Amnon Rubinstein, *Israel and the Family of Nations: The Jewish Nation-State and Human Rights*, London: Routledge, 2008; Alfred Wittstock (ed.), *The World Facing Israel—Israel Facing the World: Images and Politics*, Berlin: Frank and Timme, 2011.
17 Immanuel Kant, *The Metaphysics of Morals*, Cambridge, UK: Cambridge University Press, 1996.
18 Avraham Burg, "When the Walls Come Tumbling Down," *Haaretz*, 1 April 2011 <http://www.haaretz.com/weekend/magazine/when-the-walls-come-tumbling-down-1.353501>.
19 Ephraim Yaar and Tamar Hermann, *Peace Index-August 2010*, The Israeli Democracy Institute and Tel Aviv University <www.peaceindex.org/files/Peace%20Index-August-trans.doc>, p. 1.
20 Ibid., p. 3
21 Ibid., p. 1.
22 Levite, "It's Not the PR, Stupid."
23 Michael Bar-Zohar, *Yaacov Herzog: A Biography*, London: Halban, 2005.
24 Ibid., p. 193.
25 See also Yair Sheleg, "This is How We Ruined Toynbee's Theory," *Haaretz*, 25 August 2008 <http://www.haaretz.com/print-edition/features/this-is-how-we-ruined-toynbee-s-theory-1.210993> and Hedva Ben-Israel "Debates With Toynbee: Herzog, Talmon, Friedman", *Israel Studies*, vol. 11, no. 1, 2006, 79–90.

26 Bradley Burston, "Fear of Peace will be the Death of Israel," *Haaretz*, 3 February 2010 <http://www.haaretz.com/news/fear-of-peace-will-be-the-death-of-israel-1.262696>.

27 Friedrich Nietzsche, *Beyond Good and Evil: Prelude to a Philosophy of the Future*, Cambridge: Cambridge University Press, 2001.

28 Martin Buber, *Israel and the World: Essays in a Time of Crisis*, Syracuse NY: Syracuse University Press, 1997.

29 I thank Howard Adelman for incisive comments on my hypotheses.

30 Buber, *Israel and the World*, pp. 224–6.

31 Ibid., pp. 221, 226.

32 Interview with Bernard Avishai, *The Agenda with Steve Paiken*, 13 April 2010 <http://www.youtube.com/watch?v=gCHWJj4OaHw&feature=related>.

33 Peter Beinart, "The Failure of the American Jewish Establishment," *New York Review of Books*, 10 June 2010 <http://www.nybooks.com/articles/archives/2010/jun/10/failure-american-jewish-establishment/>. See also Peter Beinart, *The Crisis of Zionism*, New York: Holt, Henry and Co., Times Books, 2012.

34 Nadav G. Shelef, *Evolving Nationalism: Homeland, Identity, and Religion in Israel*, Ithaca, NY: Cornell University Press, 2010.

35 Emanuel Adler, "Evolving Nationalisms and the Future of Zionism," paper presented at the 27th meeting of the Association for Israel Studies, Brandeis University, 13–15 June 2011.

36 A. B. Yehoshua, "Why the Israeli–Palestinian Conflict Refuses to be Resolved," *Haaretz*, 26 April 2011 <http://www.haaretz.com/print-edition/features/why-the-israeli-palestinian-conflict-refuses-to-be-resolved-1.358095>.

2 The State of Israel and the Negation of the Exile

Michael Walzer

Given the way that Israel is embattled in the world today, this is probably an occasion when one ought to say good things about it. One ought to respond to efforts by European intellectuals, and others too, to deny legitimacy to the Jewish state. And there are many good things to say, and easy arguments to make in defense of Israel's legitimacy. In a world of failed states, tyrannical states, terrorist states, and morally bankrupt states that lend support to the tyrants and terrorists, Israel is a model of democracy. Even those of us who strongly oppose its policies in the occupied territories can recognize the difference between this state and most of the others.

But I come out of a Jewish tradition of anxiety and self-criticism (which is not the same as anger and self-hatred), and so I am going to worry with you, or at least in front of you, about some features of Jewish history that have made statehood harder and more problematic than it might have been. These are Zionist worries, and they serve to explain why the project of "negating the exile" was and still is an absolutely necessary project—though I will also worry, in a characteristically Jewish way, that negation can sometimes be too successful, can sometimes be carried too far.

Let me begin with a central issue of political life: the necessity, if you have a state, of ruling over others, over strangers, resident aliens, new immigrants, national and religious minorities, conquered peoples. This isn't an issue only in imperial states like the old Soviet Union or the British Empire, but in all states, including the Jewish state. The US rules over Indian tribes. The Norwegians rule over the Lapps and now over Macedonians and Turks. The Italians rule over immigrant Albanians, the French over immigrant Algerians, the Egyptians over Copts, the Turks over Kurds, the Chinese over Muslim tribesmen, and so on.

In the long centuries of the exile, in all of the Diaspora, the Jews ruled only over themselves; we ruled only over ourselves—when we ruled at all. The autonomous or semi-autonomous communities, the kehillot of Ashkenaz and of Spain and North Africa and the Ottoman empire and Poland, Hungary, and Russia, were radically homogeneous; they consisted only of Jews. Good Jews and bad Jews, no doubt—but, as Rashi said (citing Tractate Sanhedrin), bad Jews are still Jews; they do not become "other."[1] Even the *herem* (ostracism or excommunication) did not create otherness in the *kahal*, since its point was to force compliance with communal norms, to bring people back, not to exclude them permanently.

So the Jews were responsible only for the well-being of the Jews, while our gentile rulers were responsible for all the people they ruled, including the Jews. They were never reliably responsible—we all know the history—but we often turned to them for protection (against populist preachers and murderous mobs in the Middle Ages, for example), and sometimes, at least, we were protected. In many of the exilic communities, we counted on the gentile rulers to protect us even from our own criminals: they took charge of corporal and capital punishment—and we were not unhappy to surrender that ugly work. Jewish writers sometimes claimed that we were too good to exercise political power, even for our own protection—you can find the twentieth-century philosophical version of this idea in Franz Rosenzweig and the religious version in Abraham Isaac Kook.[2] We weren't brutal enough, so we looked for protection to the people who were brutal enough. (But I should remind you of Judah Halevi's comment on this question. In his *Kuzari*, the Rabbi tells the Khazar king that the Jews have a closer relation to God than do the nations that "flog and slay, whose power and might are great, whose walls are strong, and whose chariots are terrible." The king responds: "This might be so if your humility were voluntary, but it is involuntary, and if you had power you would [flog and] slay." And the Rabbi responds: "You have touched our weak spot.")[3]

But what is most important for my argument today is that no one, no group of "others," looked to us, to our power and might, for protection. Though Jews are enjoined in the Talmud to visit the gentile sick and help the gentile poor, that is for the sake of peace, not because we were in any political sense responsible for their sick or poor; nor did they ever count on our help or argue that they were entitled to it.

Think of that as part of what it means to be stateless. We were never without communal institutions, but these were radically our own; they gave us some power, to collect taxes and to organize welfare services, for example, but only for ourselves. States have a wider reach. This is obvious in the case of autocratic regimes, where the autocrat is responsible for all his subjects (not just for his relatives, though most autocratic rulers privilege their relatives). But even in democratic regimes, where the citizens are collectively responsible for themselves, they are not responsible only for themselves. They have obligations with regard to everyone who lives within the borders of the state. In the US, the Supreme Court has made itself the protector of powerless minorities among American citizens and also, very importantly, of foreign residents, insisting that aliens have rights and monitoring how officials of the executive branch deal with them. Today, the issues that the Court addresses arise everywhere; all states are radically pluralist, and all governments are responsible for some set of "others."

As I've suggested, Jews counted on responsible rulers, though we were more often in the position of begging for protection than of claiming it as our due. Thus, the ancient prayer for the king, adapted in some orthodox congregations in the US into a prayer for the president, which expresses the hope that he "will deal kindly with us."[4] An odd thing to be asking of a president who has to ask us for our votes, but it is evidence of the exilic state of mind. I want to stress, again, that, in the years of the exile, no one ever asked us to deal kindly with them.

Being responsible for the common good of a pluralist society, for the well-being of strangers, for all the "others," takes getting used to. It is a feature of political life, not of personal or familial or communal life. We may contribute, privately, personally, to charitable organizations (like the American Jewish World Service) that help people whom we don't know, in near or faraway places, but we aren't responsible for them. We hope that they do well; we hope that our contribution is of some use to them. But if not, not—and then we will say that there is nothing more that we can do. When we answer "yes" to the question, "Am I my brother's keeper?" we usually have in mind a parochial notion of the brethren whom we have to keep. In politics, however, the people we have to keep are not only our brethren. Though the reach of the state isn't universal, it extends well beyond family and ethnic kin.

In late 1947, when the Jews of Palestine were about to enter the society of states, David Ben-Gurion spoke to a meeting of Mapai (the ancestor of the Labor Party) about the responsibilities that came with statehood. This is what he said:

> We must think in terms of a state, in terms of independence, in terms of full responsibility for ourselves—and for others. In our state there will be non-Jews as well, and all of them will be equal citizens, equal in everything without any exception; that is, the state will be their state as well. The attitude of the Jewish State to its Arab citizens will be an important factor—though not the only one—in building good neighborly relations with the Arab States. The striving for a Jewish–Arab alliance requires us to fulfill several obligations [this is Ben-Gurion's invocation of "the ways of peace," but he then goes on], *which we are obliged to do in any event*: full and real equality, de jure and de facto, of all the state's citizens, gradual equalization of the economic, social, and cultural standard of living of the Arab community with the Jewish community; recognition of the Arabic language as the language of the Arab citizens in the administration, courts of justice, and above all in schools; municipal autonomy in villages and cities, and so on.[5]

Ben-Gurion was certainly too optimistic about the possibility of a Jewish–Arab alliance, and more than a little presumptuous in including "culture" in his talk of equalization. Nor did he, and the governments he later led, live up to the commitments he described here. Nonetheless, this was the language of a statesman—in the literal sense of that word: a man who understood what it would mean to have a state, to be "enstated" in the world. And it was critically important for him to give this speech, precisely because the responsibilities of statehood were so new to the people he was addressing.

Well, not entirely new, and here perhaps Ben-Gurion's attachment to ancient Jewish history and his intense dislike for the exilic years, his own desire to "negate the exile," served him well (although it didn't always do that). He remembered that David's kingdom, as it is described in the Bible, included not only non-Judahite tribes but also non-Israelite nations: it was pluralist in the old imperial style, even if the imperium was very small. We have no information about how the other nations were treated, though some of their members seem to have served in David's army. Remember Uriah the Hittite, who did not fare well, and Ittai the Gittite, who did. Many centuries later, the Hasmoneans extended their rule over foreign nations. We know that one of these, the Idumeans, the former Edomites, were forcibly converted to Judaism, but other groups apparently were left to their own devices, so that there was a substantial non-Jewish population in the land when the Romans conquered it. Exactly what political responsibility meant in those days is unclear. But, in Tractate Avodah Zarah, the rabbis allow the Romans to claim that they have indeed taken responsibility for the well-being of the Jews. Asked by God what they can say for themselves, the Romans reply: "Master of the Universe, we have established numerous *fora* (forums), built numerous bath houses, generated an abundance of silver and gold—and all this we did for the sake of Israel, so that they could occupy themselves with the Torah." The rabbis dispute this claim, providing a critical, anti-imperialist account of Rome's supposed benefits, but, even as they deny the Roman claim, they clearly understand what it means to act responsibly—or at least what it means for the gentiles.[6] They probably don't imagine that Jews can act in that way; they are already stateless, living in exile.

Ben-Gurion realized that the Jews, even his Jews, the Zionist vanguard, the leaders of Mapai, had no experience ruling over others, and he also realized that this is something that has to be learned. There is no reason to think that it comes naturally. Domination may (or may not) come naturally; responsibility for distant others, people who aren't part of the family, certainly doesn't. It is a political virtue, and we find it best understood (which doesn't mean best enacted) in long-established political elites. The old aristocracy cultivated a sense of service to the lower orders, even when they were actually exploiting them; they knew what it meant to protect the "others," and the claim that they in fact provided protection was their legitimizing ideology. Once the modern state was founded, aristocratic families sent many of their children into the higher civil service, and some of those civil servants really did serve the common good. After emancipation, some Jews entered the world of the aristocracy and the civil service, but only in very small numbers and usually at a price: these were assimilated Jews, sometimes converts to Christianity.[7] They imitated their gentile rulers; they didn't produce a specifically Jewish awareness of what I will now call civic responsibility—which is what I think Ben-Gurion meant, or part of what he meant, or was trying to get at, by the Hebrew word *mamlachtiyut*. The word is usually translated "statism," but I think that "civism" gives us a better sense of Ben-Gurion's argument.[8]

Civism is precisely the acceptance of responsibility for the general welfare. Jean-Jacques Rousseau provides a good account of what that requires when he writes that citizens, when they are voting, should ask not only "What's good for me or for my group?" (What's good for the middle class, for the steelworkers, for old people, for the Jews?) but also "What's good for the country?" They have an interest in the common good—which is also the good of people other than the ones they know.[9]

Now consider a true story about Israel today (or just a decade ago). In 1999, I was in Jerusalem on sabbatical, and one day I read in *Haaretz* a fascinating story about the Minister of Labor, a Shas minister in Bibi Netanyahu's first government, who had brought a suit against a restaurant in Eilat for violating the law about employing Jews on Shabbat. The restaurant was fined NIS 200,000. It appealed, and the district court judge reduced the fine to NIS 18 and castigated the minister for what I will call a violation of the norm of *mamlachtiyut*. He had brought many suits of this kind, the judge said, but not a single suit aimed at enforcing the laws against child labor, or the factory safety laws, or the laws protecting foreign workers, or any other of the laws that one would have thought to be his special responsibility. Ministerial office for him was simply an occasion to advance the projects of his own religious group. He had no sense of being responsible for a state, of being responsible for the well-being of all the citizens of the state—and for non-citizens too, who lived and worked within the state's borders. I am sure that he was a good Jew, but he was a Jew of the *galut* (and of the pre-emancipation *galut*), lost in what must be for him a totally unexpected state—a Jewish state with a substantial percentage of non-Jewish citizens. Who ever heard of such a thing?

So we have to hear—and think—about such things. And perhaps we also have to learn from the experience of other democratic states, which have, not without ongoing difficulty, accommodated the strangers in their midst. There is another issue that comes with statehood and that also requires learning from the others: the need to argue about and to decide when to go to war and how to fight. The Jewish tradition is radically deficient here, and the deficiency, again, has a Zionist explanation. Adequate theoretical accounts of when to fight and how to fight are written by citizens of states that actually have to make decisions about these questions. And for almost 2000 years, from the time of Bar Kokhba to the time of Ben-Gurion, the Jews did not have states of that sort. We were often the victims in gentile wars; we were not the agents of Jewish wars. One might expect that victims would produce their own accounts of what should and shouldn't happen in wartime. I suggest reading Maimonides' famous line about siege warfare—that cities should only be surrounded on three sides, so that trapped civilians can get out—as an example of the victim's view.[10] But victims more often produce dirges and laments, chronicles of death and destruction; they don't write moral treatises. The truth is that Jewish (halakhic) arguments about the morality of war are very thin.

On the question of when to fight, the rabbis worked with the two ideas of commandment and permission. We have to fight when God commands us (as in the original conquest of the land), and we are permitted to fight, or, better, a Jewish king is permitted to fight, as Maimonides writes, "to extend the borders of Israel and to enhance his greatness and prestige" (the immediate reference is to David's wars). There are rabbis in Israel today who think that both the command and the permission still apply—and some of these are chaplains in the Israel Defense Forces (IDF). Until fairly recently, this twofold classification was not extended to its natural third: prohibited wars. One reason for this is obvious: according to the moral standards that have prevailed for centuries in both the Jewish and Christian worlds, the wars of extermination commanded in Deuteronomy would have to be prohibited. The rabbis could not do that; they had to find other ways of nullifying the command-ments. But without that third category, there can't be an explicit and coherent debate about when it is or isn't right to fight—or, in a different theoretical language, when war is just and when it is unjust. Before 1948, Jews as Jews, in a Jewish state, did not have to debate this question.

For the same reason, we did not have to debate the many issues that arise in the course of battle. How should soldiers aim their weapons? Who is it right to kill, or try to kill, and who must be shielded from combat? What risks must soldiers take in order to minimize the risks they impose on non-combatants? What degree of collateral damage is permissible? Jewish writers don't have much to say about these questions because, until 1948 again, we didn't have soldiers fighting in a Jewish army who needed answers. As J. David Bleich has written (I wouldn't trust myself to make such a strong assertion), "there exists no discussion in classical rabbinic sources that takes cognizance of the likelihood of causing civilian casualties in the course of hostilities legitimately undertaken as posing a halakhic or moral problem."[11] Rabbi Bleich writes a hard sentence; what he means is that collateral damage, unintended civilian death, whatever its extent, is not recognized as morally problematic by the classical Jewish authorities. That makes sense: historically, it wasn't their moral problem—but now it is ours. And many of Israel's rabbis are still addressing it in the old way, as if civilian deaths, especially if the civilians are non-Jews, are not problematic in any way.

Of course, secular Israelis are debating these issues in the languages of international law and just war theory—the latter the creation of Catholic moral theologians, who had a lot of states and a lot of armies in the field, over many centuries. These are important debates, but they don't sufficiently engage the religious sector of Israeli society, whose members often regard arguments about just and unjust wars, and even arguments about "the purity of arms," as non-Jewish or even anti-Jewish. The secularists, on the other hand, have so successfully negated the exile that they can't engage, even critically engage, with exilic Judaism or, specifically, with the halakha of war. They can't, so to speak, naturalize international law and just war theory within the Jewish tradition, since they don't know the tradition, and so they can't argue in a useful way with their religious fellow-citizens. And some process of that sort, of the naturalizing sort, will be necessary if Israeli Jews are to do two things that are critically important, politically and morally: to learn from the wisdom of foreigners and to speak to one another.

I want to finish by addressing one more feature of statehood for which Jewish history provided no preparation—that is, the experience of formulating and arguing about foreign policy. In the centuries of exile, *stadlanut* was our foreign policy—the work of the *stadlan*, the court Jew, the intermediary, who pleaded on our behalf for the protection of our gentile overlords, asking them to "deal kindly with us."[12] The literature of *stadlanut* is not attractive; it is a literature of humiliation, and reading it will make your skin crawl; it provides a very strong argument for Zionism and statehood. The men who pleaded for protection (Queen Esther is the only woman I know of in this role) acted in private; what they said was never the subject of public or democratic discussion; mostly, Jews didn't want to know what the pleading entailed. Everyone's assumption was that the gentiles were always and everywhere hostile; that's why it was necessary for some well-placed and wealthy person to beg, to grovel, to bribe. This was nothing like a relationship of respect and equality.

But statehood and then membership in the international society of states does bring us into a relationship of (formal) equality—despite the obvious differences in state power. Now we have to relate not to the exilic but to the biblical *goyim*—that is, to other nations that have the same standing that Israel has. It is natural, I suppose, to carry over to this new relationship the old state of mind: "The whole world is on one side, and we are on the other." This grim sentence has been repeated again and again, not only in the Diaspora, where it might have some point, in some places, but also in contemporary Israel, where it is an astonishing misperception of the actual state of international politics. The sense of being persecuted, hated, isolated, and embattled is not a good foundation, psychological or strategic, for the diplomatic and military engagements that statehood makes possible ... and necessary.

For the truth is that Israel is engaged, very much like a normal state, with friends and enemies. Right now, Israel has a lot of enemies, most of whom, thank heaven, are capable only of rhetorical hostility; but it also has important friends, whose value many of its citizens, and some of its leaders, seriously underestimate. Many years ago, I heard a very smart student of international politics say that we would know that Zionism had been a success when Israel became a full partner in the local politics of alliance and enmity. That happened in 1970, when the IDF defended Jordanian sovereignty against a Syrian threat. Ever since that time, Israel has been involved in Middle Eastern alliance politics; it is involved today, and it has strategic allies among its neighbors, even if these allies are not quite friends. But the "All the world is against us" mentality makes it unnecessarily hard to develop and improve upon these connections—unnecessarily hard to make prudential judgments about friends and enemies. Too many Israelis live in their still new state as if they were still in exile. Once again, I think that this is especially so among religious Jews, but the carryover of exilic attitudes affects secularists also.

Israeli Jews need to deal with all these issues: ruling over others, fighting wars (and criticizing the wars and the fighting), forging alliances in the society of states. And what is necessary in each case, or what is necessary to get started, is a critical engagement with Jewish history and with the Jewish tradition, that is, with the legal and philosophical literature of the exile. The engagement has to be critical because exile makes for pathology. That's another Zionist argument, though perhaps "pathology" is not quite the right word. It might be better to say that a history that did not include looking after the welfare of others; arguing about when, and when not, to fight; and dealing with friends as well as enemies—that is a deficient history and a bad preparation for independence and statehood.

But there is also much that I haven't talked about today: the remarkable solidarity of the exile, its capacity for repeated regeneration, and the tough realism of its fearfulness. None of these is pathological. That's why it isn't only criticism but also engagement that is necessary. Statehood wasn't the great awakening that Zionists sometimes described, because we weren't sleeping in the years of exile; we were busy surviving. Sovereignty is supposed to make survival easier, but there is a necessary educational process here, which is well begun but far from finished: Jews have to learn what it means to be sovereign and how sovereignty is best enacted in a world of states.

Notes

1 Rashi, *Responsa* 175; BT Sanhedrin 44a. See Michael Walzer, Menachem Lorberbaum, Noam Zohar (eds), *The Jewish Political Tradition*, vol. 2: *Membership*, New Haven, CT: Yale University Press, 2003, pp. 334–5.
2 Franz Rosenzweig, *The Star of Redemption*, trans. William W. Hallo, Notre Dame, IN: University of Notre Dame Press, 1985, pp. 328–35; Abraham Isaac Kook, *Orot*, trans. Bezalel Naor, Northvale, NJ: Jacob Aronson, 1993, p. 96.
3 Judah Halevi, *The Kuzari*, trans. Hartwig Hirschfeld, New York: Schocken, 1964, pp. 78–9.
4 See Walzer, Lorberbaum, and Zohar, *The Jewish Political Tradition: Membership*, pp. 516–19.
5 Quoted in Efraim Karsh, *Fabricating Israeli History: The "New Historians,"* London: Frank Cass, 1997, p. 67.
6 BT Avodah Zarah, 2a–3b.
7 See, for example, the recent biography of Walter Rathenau by Shulamit Volkov: *Weimar's Fallen Statesman*, New Haven, CT: Yale University Press, 2012.
8 See Nir Kedar, "Ben-Gurion's *Mamlakhtiyut*: Etymological and Theoretical Roots," *Israel Studies*, vol. 7, no. 3, Fall 2003, 117–33.
9 Rousseau, *The Social Contract*, Book 3, chapter 15.
10 Maimonides, *Mishneh Torah*, The Book of Judges, Treatise Five, Kings and Wars, 6:7.
11 J. David Bleich, "Pre-emptive War in Jewish Law," *Tradition*, vol. 21, no. 1, Spring 1983, 8–9.
12 For a useful historical account, see David Biale, *Power and Powerlessness in Jewish History*, New York: Schocken, 1986.

3 Cosmopolitanism

Good for Israel? Or Bad for Israel?

Michael Barnett

Many supporters of Israel exclaim that the world increasingly questions Israel's legitimacy, treats Israel as a pariah state, and exhibits little sympathy when the country and its citizens are attacked. Assuming their observations are founded, the question is: why? There is a range of candidate explanations. Israel has failed to do what it can and must do to make peace with the Palestinians. It is a by-product of Israel's impossible situation—it has no one with whom to make a real peace, and so is forced to play occupier in an age where occupiers are reviled and the occupied are automatically granted underdog status. The world has forgotten the Holocaust and is increasingly anti-Semitic. Western states are following their domestic and strategic interests—away from Israel. European states contain a growing vocal and radicalized Muslim minority that makes noise in the streets and at the polls. And Israel no longer serves Western strategic interests the way it once did during the Cold War. It has always been tough being Israel, but now more so than ever.

This essay explores another possibility: the character of contemporary cosmopolitanism coupled with an Israel that increasingly sees itself (and is seen) as a "people apart." This argument has four corners. The first is cosmopolitanism. The world has become increasingly cosmopolitan. Certainly not to the point that nationalism and national identities are archaic expressions of a pre-globalized era, but certainly to the point that citizens of one country worry about the fates and circumstances of the citizens of other countries. Cosmopolitanism is not new and it comes in many different forms. After the Second World War, though, a cosmopolitanism of suffering became the defining expression of our identification with distant others. This cosmopolitanism of suffering is most evident in duties to aid, responsibilities to protect, and a right to be protected from unnecessary harm. Although a cosmopolitanism of suffering is organized around the principle of humanity, as a cosmopolitanism dedicated to the alleviation of unnecessary suffering, it is also organized around the "victim." And in a global age where everyone is potentially a victim, it becomes even more critical to distinguish deserving from undeserving victims.

The second cornerstone concerns the relationship between cosmopolitanism and the Jews. Jews have often been seen by others as the quintessential cosmopolitans. Whether this was to their benefit or detriment, though, has depended on whether the broader community sees cosmopolitanism as friend or foe. Political projects that favor exclusion over inclusion—especially evident during the age of nationalism in the nineteenth century—have treated the Jews as "rootless cosmopolitans," who have dual loyalties and are a threat to the nation. Political projects that favor inclusion over exclusion—especially evident during the age of liberal nationalism and after the Second World War when internationalism meant an international community based on humanity—have welcomed Jews as equal citizens and recognized them as having equal moral worth. Yet whether cosmopolitanism is good for the Jews or bad for the Jews depends on the form of really, existing cosmopolitanism. I will argue that, while a cosmopolitanism of suffering initially favored the Jews and Israel, it no longer does. But the story does not end there. Equally important is how Jewish communities answer the "Jewish Question": whether, how, and should Jews maintain their identity in the world? Jews have asked this question over the millennium, and their responses have depended on time, place, and political culture. Sometimes Jews have seen themselves as part of this world, at other times as a people apart.

The third corner examines how Israel has produced different blends of particularism and universalism, thus answering the Jewish Question not in reference to itself (after all, it is a state dedicated to Jewish existence) but rather in relationship to the broader (non-Jewish) world. There is a general consensus of opinion that Israel's political culture relies less on forms of universalism and more on forms of particularism, sometimes nationalist and sometimes religious. This growing sense of being a "people apart," though, has been accompanied by a growing assertion that Israel is a victim, particularly evident in the public use of and reference to the Holocaust. These three corners lead to the fourth: the same world that expresses a cosmopolitanism of suffering also has more difficulty accepting that Israel is a victim, for some quite obvious and some less obvious reasons. There is a growing gap between a cosmopolitanism of suffering, on the one hand, and an Israel that increasingly presents itself as being a "people apart."

We live in a world not only of victims but also of victimhood, where the victims' identity is defined by their suffering. Israel is often accused of being pathologically attached to the identity of victim. In the conclusion, I want to consider how my argument regarding the relationship between a cosmopolitanism of suffering and Israel's standing as a victim address this controversial, polemical, and ultimately irresolvable debate. Although one person's pathological attachment to a victim identity can be another person's sober recognition, and historical experience, that the world is sometimes out to get you, I want to suggest that Israel's sense of being a "people apart" might be both a cause and effect of its sense of victimization.

Cosmopolitanism

Cosmopolitanism's meanings have changed over the centuries and with the times, though several are most important for contemporary discussions. The Stoics of ancient Greece are credited with its initial use; they imagined widening the individual's relationship from the polis to the cosmos and all of humanity. Immanuel Kant added an additional layer that included public reasoning. Its enlightenment-influenced significance is the claim that all people have moral worth and a right to participate in the "global community of argument."[1] Everyone deserves consideration in public dialogue and debate. A third, more recent and common, meaning is that all human beings have equal worth and basic rights, and that we have obligations to those who are distant strangers, especially when their security, dignity and rights are threatened. Principles of humanity and impartiality are central to this more recent vision of cosmopolitanism.

A cosmopolitanism that pivots on principles of humanity, impartiality, and mutual recognition must confront, both in theory and in practice, the question of diversity. Central to notions of cosmopolitanism is the belief that our common humanity means that we have shared values and basic needs, and are equally entitled to basic human rights. But our humanity, in its fullest sense, is created by history and culture. If we reduce humanity to uniform attributes, what sort of humanity is this? Does cosmopolitanism demand that we flatten diversity? At this moment, defenders of cosmopolitanism offer two defenses. One is that there are "thin" and "thick" versions of cosmopolitanism, and thin versions try to find our common elements while recognizing that there is considerable cultural variation that also deserves respect and tolerance. The second defense is to insist that cosmopolitanism demands more than mere tolerance—it also requires that we be prepared to learn from difference.[2]

The concerns regarding the relationship between diversity and unity, particularism and universalism, are central to the debate regarding the relationship between nationalism and cosmopolitanism. Because cosmopolitanism holds that our loyalties and commitments should not be exhausted by existing group divisions, a central question is whether cosmopolitanism represents a threat to nationalism or whether the two can get along. There is certainly no agreed-upon position, either in principle or fact. Much depends on what versions of nationalism and cosmopolitanism are under consideration. Versions of nationalism that are based on blood, belonging, language, tribe, ethnicity, religion, and other kinds of exclusive markers are more likely to see cosmopolitanism as not only a rival but also a threat. Versions of nationalism that are more liberally minded, and thus do not engage in any profiling before considering membership and citizenship, are less likely to see cosmopolitanism as an immediate threat. But much also depends on the character of cosmopolitanism. A cosmopolitanism that aspires to replace the world of nation-states with a single, sovereignty polity will be seen as a direct competitor. However, a cosmopolitanism that does not imagine unifying borders but is satisfied ensuring that individual rights and needs are met—in the first instance by the state and in the second instance by the international community—will not pose the same threat to state sovereignty. The broader point, then, is that cosmopolitanism is attached to different kinds of political projects—world federalism; communism; human rights; religious unity; and a duty to relieve the suffering of others—which have very different relationships to, and make very different demands on, states and their citizens.

At the risk of gross historical simplification, over the last 150 years, the relationship between nationalism and cosmopolitanism has gone through two periods. The first period began with the rise of modern nationalism in the nineteenth century and peaked with the First and Second World Wars. During this period, in which states were undergoing the difficult process of nation-building and were trying to subsume existing local and transnational identities to the national state, cosmopolitanism was seen as a rival and threat— as were those who were identified as communists, Bolsheviks, socialists, and anarchists. But not all forms of cosmopolitanism were immediately put on a watch list. Many evangelical Christians, including those who saw communism as a Godless scourge, believed in the unity of all humans and championed missionary projects in order to help bring about that unity. The second period began with the Great Wars of the last century. Nationalism was seen as a major cause of rivalry and violence, and the challenge became how to civilize nationalism. Although some political projects looked no further than advocating enlightened self-interest, others championed an international community based on a common humanity and the shared dignity of all peoples. Whereas during the age of nationalism cosmopolitanism was often seen as a diabolical threat, in the age of international community it became a saving idea.

Cosmopolitanism comes in many different forms, and after the Second World War there emerged a cosmopolitanism of suffering. We begin with a thin notion of cosmopolitanism, one based on the belief that all humans are of equal moral worth and have basic human rights. But when, precisely, do we identify with those on the other side of political, religious, cultural, and territorial borders? Moments of violence, pain, cruelties, indignities, and unnecessary suffering have the capacity to lead one people to identify with the circumstances and recognize the humanity of another people. The First and Second World Wars, the Holocaust, and every succeeding humanitarian nightmare gave greater moral weight to cosmopolitanism, fueled by images transported by new visual technologies that made people aware of suffering when it was occurring and shocking them into action.[3] Sentiments of cosmopolitan became institutionalized in an international humanitarian order that is dedicated to the relief of unnecessary suffering, present in global documents and organizations, including the Universal Declaration of Human Rights and the Geneva Convention, and evident in areas such as emergency relief, development, human rights, and public health.[4] Importantly, then, postwar cosmopolitanism is a cosmopolitanism of suffering. Although it is formed in part by notions of humanity and other levelers of difference, in fact it divides the world into two: those who are sufferers and depend on others to recognize their right not to suffer; and those who are responsible for ministering relief. This is not a solidarity based on friendship or even civic equality, but instead is based on inequities and potentially leads, as Hannah Arendt warned, to a "politics of pity."

Victims stand at the center of this cosmopolitan world. The concept of victim did not circulate widely until the seventeenth century when it came to mean a "living creature sacrificed to a deity" (which is also consistent with the biblical Hebrew term *korben*), and thus had a religious meaning, and a century later took on the added dimension of someone who suffers acute loss.[5] This is a world that increasingly recognizes the pain of others and wants to do something to relieve and compensate them for their suffering.

This development can be viewed charitably or uncharitably. We could see this as a sign of moral progress, evidence that we have truly globalized notions of humanity to include everyone. We also could worry that we have entered into an age of global victimhood.[6] Anyone who has ever suffered a loss of one sort or another can claim to be a victim. What has produced this worldwide craze? Although discourses of humanity deserve credit, there are some slightly more cynical explanations. It has become a way of asserting one's identity, especially one's authenticity in a globalizing age in which we are in danger of becoming faceless.[7] People want to be classified as victims because, only then, will they get social recognition and be entitled to special assistance. This certainly helps explain the ascendance of victims' rights movements in the postwar period. The rise of global victimhood alongside the proliferation of victims' rights movements has led to an "Olympics of Suffering."[8] Different groups now compete for the distinction of the world's greatest victim. Importantly, this competition is even open to those who caused other people's suffering: perpetrators can be victims. According to Didier Fassin and Richard Rechtman, a decisive turning point for transforming perpetrators into victims occurred with the Vietnam War, when returning American soldiers were treated as victims with PTSD not because of the suffering they endured but because of the atrocities they inflicted.[9]

Among the consequences of this growth of victimhood, two are most relevant for a cosmopolitanism of suffering. One, there has been a corresponding desire to distinguish "true," "innocent," and "deserving" victims from all the rest. To become a victim requires more than having suffered; instead, the category of "victim" is reserved for those who have certain qualities. Victims are noble and endure suffering silently. They show responsibility, accept their fate and do not use their injuries to explain their failures. They directly experienced the loss and do not claim to be a victim because of their association with a group. And they are "innocent" and thus did not contribute to their injury.[10] Second, there has been a backlash against victims.[11] They are increasingly seen as being self-absorbed, self-indulgent, and self-pitying. Some people are so consumed by their own pain and suffering that they lack empathy for others and exhibit little if any personal responsibility.[12] A world of victims means that everyone is so busy seeking others to acknowledge their pain that they have no time or ability to recognize the suffering of others.

Cosmopolitanism, Israel, and victimhood

Judaism and Jewish history are a changing composite of particularism and universalism.[13] There are enduring sentiments of particularism, captured by such expressions as a people apart, a people that dwells alone, and, most famously and controversially, a chosen people. Yet Judaism and Jewish history also contain strong elements of universalism, and even the same expressions that are offered as examples of particularism have also been invested with a universalistic interpretation. For instance, in contrast to the presumption that the "chosen people" implies distinctiveness, many reform-minded rabbis, especially those who live in liberal societies, have commented that many peoples are chosen and are chosen for different reasons, and that each can only fulfill its mission by working with others to be a "light unto nations" to create a greater unity.[14]

Jews have struggled for centuries over their relationship to the rest of the world. However, for most of their history in exile, these were theological debates with very little political import because their host communities assumed that Jews were different and could not and should not be given equal rights, treatment, or respect. However, beginning with the enlightenment, and especially with the rise of liberalism in the nineteenth century, Jews increasingly had an invitation to "integrate." But at what cost? Would integration encourage Jews to abandon Judaism altogether? Or would they "reform" to the point that their Jewish identity became meaningless and little more than a cultural attribute? If they preserved their faith and traditions, would the wider community see this as a sign of arrogance, a statement of cultural superiority, a lack of loyalty and patriotism, and a desire to remain apart?

There is no single answer to this "Jewish Question," and different Jewish communities have offered different responses. Although it is impossible to predict whether a Jewish community will be more inclined toward integration or segregation, one factor has been critical: whether the broader society honors principles of inclusion or exclusion. Where principles of inclusion such as tolerance, human dignity, and equality dominate, then questions of the price of integration become more relevant. In fact, the promise of integration can unleash a different threat to the survival of the Jewish people: assimilation. Accordingly, Jewish communities debate how to be both Jews and national citizens. In those societies where principles of exclusion that generate difference and distribute uneven rights, benefits, and opportunities dominate, then Jews are more likely to segregate, if only because they had no choice.

Such observations translate into the fairly straightforward proposition that Jews living in liberally minded societies will gravitate toward a political culture that favors universalism and those living in illiberal societies will lean to particularism. This proposition can be a guide, but it should not be completely trusted. Jews respond not only to their immediate society but also to the broader global climate. For instance, contemporary American Jewish anxieties owe less to their place in the United States and more to the attitudes prevailing in foreign lands, namely in Europe and Arab and Islamic states. In addition, Jewish communities have not only responded to their environment; they have actively attempted to shape it, as evident in the role of Jewish organizations and individuals in promoting human rights, civil rights, and open societies.[15] Jewish communities also have distinctive political cultures that are shaped by their environment, and these political cultures are "sticky," not moving lock-step with the environment. And political cultures change in response not only to external shocks but also to internal divisions.

Below I want to suggest how broad currents in cosmopolitanism shaped Israel's path to victimhood. We begin with the origins of Zionism and its relationship to the particular and the universal, with special attention to how Labor Zionism imagined normalizing the Jews and bringing them into a universalizing history. Although the Holocaust tipped the direction in favor of particularism, the early leaders of Israel ascribed to a Labor Zionism that remained hopeful that Jews and Israel would become integrated into an increasingly civilized and progressive world. Importantly, whereas prior to the Holocaust the Jewish association with cosmopolitanism was a burden, after the Holocaust it became a source of status and support; namely, Jews were second to none in a world of suffering. Yet, because of a dominant strand of Zionist thought, Israeli leaders were hardly enthusiastic about a victim identity.

After 1967, the forces favoring particularism gained ground in Israel. Alongside the rise of particularism was a greater willingness by Israeli leaders to present Israel as a victim, but this was also the moment when the world became increasingly skeptical of its case.The age of nationalism in Europe, Eastern Europe, and Russia in the nineteenth century gave birth to Zionism. Jews had it relatively good in countries like France, England, and Germany where liberal nationalism was taking root. Liberalism and secularization were combining with nationalism to produce discourses of dignity, equality, and citizenship. Yet it is important not to romanticize this development. If Jews were doing relatively well in post-enlightenment Western Europe, it was only in comparison to the Jewish condition historically and in other parts of Europe. Even revolutionary France, the first European country to grant citizenship to Jews, could not imagine that the Jews would ever become truly French. They were said to lack the proper "relationship to French soil" and tradition, their wandering ways meant that they could not claim roots in France, or anywhere else for that matter, and they might corrupt French heritage.[16] They were welcome to try, but it would depend mightily on their willingness to abandon their Jewish nationality in favor of French nationality. As Count Stanislas de Clermont-Tonnerre declared in 1789 on the occasion of the debate in the French National Assembly regarding the emancipation of the Jews: "It is necessary to refuse everything to the Jews as a nation and grant the Jews everything as individuals."[17] For the Jews of Europe, this was progress. In contrast to France and other liberalizing regions of Europe that were prepared to see the Jews as reformable, much of the rest of Europe was nationalizing without liberalizing, and with severe consequences for the Jews. As the ultimate outsider, in these countries, Jews faced discrimination, prejudice, restrictions to jobs and education, and pogroms.[18]

These nationalist conditions produced Zionism and those regions in Europe that had nationalism without liberalism were precisely where Zionism gained the strongest following. There were various branches of Zionism, which presented different mixtures of universalism and particularism. Labor Zionism, the version that dominated Jewish Palestine and influenced Israel's founding figures, imagined a nationalism that worked with cosmopolitanism. All of the major branches of Zionism believed that Jewish survival and security could not depend on the *goyim*. But Labor Zionism wanted to do more than simply provide a safe haven for Jews. It also wanted to "normalize" them. Why were the Jews abnormal? Partly because they were a nation without political sovereignty; a national homeland, therefore, was essential to their normalization. Exile was an unfortunate fate that could only be remedied by the return to Israel. As David Ben-Gurion said,

> Each of us stands in awe and deep admiration before the tremendous emotional power revealed by the Jews in their wanderings and sufferings in the diaspora. I will admire any man who is sick and in pain and who struggles for his survival, who does not bow to his bitter fate, but I will not consider his to be an ideal condition. In contrast, the builders of the State of Israel rebelled against the lack of Jewish independence and freedom that characterized Jewish history in exile.[19]

The consequence of exile, however, affected more than the Jews' physical security—it also distorted the Jewish character. In fact, much of Zionist ideology possessed a rather uncharitable, almost classically anti-Semitic, view of the *galut* (Jews in exile). Centuries of exile and persecution had left the Jews emotionally, psychologically, culturally, and physically crippled. Consider the rest of Ben-Gurion's statement, as he negates the exile with reference to the classic anti-Semitic character Shylock:

> I do not despise Shylock for making his living from usury. He had no other choice in the place of his exile, and in his quality of morality, he stood far above the grand lords who humiliated him; but I will not turn Shylock into an ideal and man of stature whom I seek to emulate. The Jews of the Diaspora are not Shylocks—but it is difficult to accommodate the glorification of life in the Diaspora with the ideal that seventy years ago was given the name "Zionism." As a rejector of the *galut*, I reject the glorification of the *galut*.[20]

Ben-Gurion simultaneously rejects the characterization of Jews as Shylocks and insinuates that they possessed some of his traits. These unsavory characteristics stemmed not from anything intrinsic to Judaism or Jews, but rather to centuries of life under foreign rule. Jews in the *galut* had a victim mentality, cowardly, cowering, and passive. When news of the Holocaust reached the Yishuv leaders, they were certainly shocked by its barbarism but they believed the rumors that Jews had been going like sheep to their deaths because this was what they expected from *galut* Jews. Zionism would not just end exile—it would negate it. The end of exile and the acquisition of political and military power in a framework of sovereignty would purge the fact and stereotype of the "submissible cowardly Jew."[21] Jews would not only get respect, they would earn it.

Although Zionism was a response to a long history of anti-Semitism, and thus saw Jews as victims, Zionism had little patience for a victim identity.[22] A sense of victimhood was part and parcel of a *galut* attitude. Zionism, on the other hand, wanted to expel such contemptible traits and sense of fatalism, and, instead, cultivate a culture of agency. Zionists were men and women of action, courage, and determination, traits that were foreign to *galut* Jews. Yishuv leaders were so convinced of this difference between themselves and Jews in the Diaspora that, when they learned of Jewish resistance during the Holocaust in general and the Warsaw ghetto uprising in particular, they credited themselves as a source of inspiration.[23] When Masada was originally proposed as possible source material for the Yishuv collective identity, Ben-Gurion reportedly answered that he did not believe that a story that ended with the decision to commit suicide rather than fight was necessarily in keeping with the Zionist image.[24]

Zionism was an answer to Jewish physical insecurity and cultural pathology, but for Labor Zionists the Jewish state would remain until world conditions changed for the better, namely, once nationalism gave way to cosmopolitanism, which would occur with the transition from capitalism to socialism. Socialist Zionists would begin the process of building socialism in Palestine, thus giving a universalizing and socialist interpretation to the notion of Jews as "chosen people." The Jewish people, in other words, would help create "the cornerstone of a new humanity and new world order."[25] In sum, the Yishuv leadership saw Zionism as having a threefold historic mission for the Jews and the world: it would provide physical security for Jews; it would help normalize the Jews by giving them a nation of their own; and the Jews would, at last, become worthy of respect.

Israel could not escape Jewish history and the recurrent question regarding how to relate the national and the universal, and the Holocaust and the cosmopolitanism of suffering intertwined to shape its composition and future.[26] As Zertal movingly writes,

> The Holocaust and its millions of dead have been ever-present in Israel from the day of its establishment and the link between the two events remains indissoluble. Through a dialectical process of appropriation and exclusion, remembering and forgetting, Israeli society has defined itself in relation to the Holocaust: it regarded itself as both the heir to the victims and their accuser, atoning for their sins and redeeming their death.[27]

Even if it had wanted to, Israel could not separate its creation and its existence from the Holocaust.[28] The issue was not only that the Holocaust and the millions of dead provided proof beyond belief of what happened when Jews relied on others for their security, but there were millions of survivors that had nowhere to go—except, perhaps, a Jewish state.

The Holocaust vindicated the importance of a Jewish state, and the Jewish state would negate the Holocaust. Israel gained considerable financial, political, and diplomatic support because of the Holocaust. It was seen by the world as the heir to the survivors and the phoenix-like symbol of the Jewish people. Although the new Israeli state benefitted from the Holocaust, the government did not entirely accept the victim identity that accompanied it, seeing itself as the symbol of Jews reborn after their near extermination.[29] Israeli leaders continued to treat the Holocaust as representative of the *galut* mentality and received survivors as pitiful reminders of a *galut* mentality that had no place in the new Israel, even callously calling them "soaps" in reference to the rumor that Germans manufactured soap from the remains of Jews.[30] The Holocaust became a point for contrast between the helpless Jews of Europe and the brave, self-reliant Jews of Israel, and a counter-metaphor for every disgraceful characteristic of Jews in exile.[31] "The establishment of Jewish sovereignty and a Jewish military force represented a revolution not only in the standing of the Jews among the nations, but also in the Jews' own image of themselves, their identity."[32] In general, Israel was both inheritor and rescuer of the Holocaust Jews, and hence Israel was the world's defining symbol of the postwar cosmopolitanism of suffering. Prior to the Second World War, Jews were symbols of cosmopolitanism, but, in an era where nationalism was valorized and cosmopolitanism demonized, Jews were the stranger, the suspect, and the stealth poison of the people. The First and Second World Wars bloodied nationalism and transformed cosmopolitanism into a saving force, and, whereas once Jews' association with cosmopolitanism was a source of violence, now it became a source of sympathy. In the postwar years, the Jews became the world's light meter—signaling whether it was trending toward dawn or night. And, as the political representative of the Jews, Israel could count on the world's sympathy, even if it did not always translate into concrete military, diplomatic, or economic support.

The 1967 war began as a replay of every nightmare of Jewish isolation and vulnerability, and ended in a Jewish fantasy. For Israel and Jews around the world, Holocaust analogies were immediate—the world was abandoning Israel at the very moment that Arab states were vowing to throw the Jews into the sea. But Israel refused to play victim or act like the Jews of Europe, and instead struck decisively and victoriously against the Arabs. Israel demonstrated that Jews could be more than victims, that Jews had learned the lesson of the Holocaust and embraced self-reliance and a willingness to use power. Israel's victory was redemptive in its fullest expression and Jews around the world burst with pride and began a genuine love affair with the Jewish state.[33]

The war was a turning point in another way: it became a moment when the Israeli political culture shifted away from liberal universalism and toward cultural distinctiveness.[34] In the first few decades, the Israeli political culture contained defining elements of liberal universalism, anchored by a Labor Zionist ideology. But, as a political project dedicated to defending Jewish security and promoting a saving Jewish identity, it also leaned toward a sense of distinctiveness. The 1967 war led to the relative elevation of cultural distinctiveness and the marginalization of liberal universalism. There were several factors at work, only some of which were directly traceable to the war itself. The failure of the international community to come to Israel's aid in its hour of need only reinforced a principal lesson of Jewish history and the Holocaust: Jews cannot and must not depend on others. The capture of the territories, and especially Jerusalem and the West Bank, unleashed heightened forms of secular nationalism and religious chauvinism.

The 1967 war also ignited the Holocaust imagery. Although constantly referenced since its founding, the post-1967 period represented a decisive break. The foundation was laid several years before at the 1961 Eichmann trial. In addition to tightening the sinews between the lessons of the Holocaust to the State of Israel, the trial also merged the Arabs with Hitler. "The trial gave new meaning to the fight against the Arab enemy and the possibility of death in this fight—the belated vindication of the fathers' helplessness in Defense of the Nazi enemy. One enemy was combined with another."[35] The Arabs replaced Hitler, and their goals toward Israel became no different from his toward the Jews. Beginning with the Eichmann trial, but then accelerating after 1967, Israel "discovered" the Holocaust and began to tie itself to it, and the Holocaust became more central to its national identity.[36] The 1967 war was replete with Holocaust references by Israeli leaders, but the 1973 war, with the very real prospect that the Arab states had successfully launched a war of annihilation, fused images of vulnerability and the Holocaust in more vividly powerful ways.

Alongside the rising importance of the Holocaust to Israel's national identity, other factors also privileged cultural particularism over liberal universalism. There was the decline of Labor Zionism, which led secular Israelis, according to Tom Segev, to turn the Holocaust into the civic religion, and paved the way for the rise of Likud, which traced its roots to a more exclusive ideology pioneered by Vladimir Jabotinsky.[37] There was the rise of religious forces. Although these were tied to different political ideologies, and there were differences of views regarding the role of religion in public life, civil and political rights, and the importance of democracy, both religious and revisionist Zionists agreed that Jews were a "people apart" and on the need for a Greater Israel.[38]

The ascendance of these forms of particularism, and the decline of Labor Zionism, *arguably* cultivated a victim identity in Israel. I want to emphasize the speculative nature of the claim because the evidence is scattered, circumstantial, and indirect at best. However, a case might form around the following leads.

To begin, there is little dispute that the Holocaust became more central to Israel's collective identity after the 1967 war. Whether this occurred because of "natural causes" or whether this was promoted strategically is in many respects beside the point—the issue is not why or how the Holocaust rose to prominence but the fact of its prominence. Second, most interpretations of the Holocaust, especially among Jews and doubly so among Israeli Jews, highlight lessons such as the importance of Jewish self-reliance, the possibility of genocidal anti-Semitism, and other reasons for the distinctiveness of the Jewish nation.[39]

Third, an analysis of Knesset debates between 1982 and 2005 lends empirical support to the claim that Israeli leaders (and presumably the Israeli Jewish public as well) identify themselves as victims.[40] We have to examine the numbers with considerable caution, especially since the content analysis begins in 1982, yet there are several interesting features. One, frequency of the usage of victims starts at a "high," declines considerably during the

Table 1 Number of Knesset Documents Containing Victimhood References

Year	Anti-Semite		Anti-Semitism		Sho'ha		Victims	
	no.	*%*	*no.*	*%*	*no.*	*%*	*no.*	*%*
1982	5	0.2	33	1.5	47	2.1	73	3.3
1983	6	0.3	18	0.8	43	1.9	82	3.6
1984	4	0.3	18	1.3	38	2.7	97	7.0
1985	6	0.2	31	1.2	90	3.6	103	4.1
1986	3	0.1	37	1.6	83	3.5	80	3.4
1987	6	0.2	24	1.0	84	3.5	90	3.7
1988	8	0.4	46	2.4	61	3.1	87	4.5
1989	3	0.1	26	1.0	89	3.3	98	3.7
1990	19	0.6	79	2.5	111	3.5	100	3.2
1991	6	0.2	65	2.0	125	3.8	114	3.4
1992	5	0.3	25	1.3	60	3.1	79	4.0
1993	2	0.1	38	1.0	109	2.9	146	3.9
1994	10	0.2	45	1.0	114	2.5	188	4.1
1995	8	0.2	37	1.0	113	3.0	164	4.4
1996	5	0.2	31	1.2	67	2.5	113	4.3
1997	4	0.1	30	0.8	116	3.1	133	3.5
1998	7	0.2	51	1.2	109	2.6	124	2.9
1999	10	0.6	35	2.1	79	4.8	96	5.8
2000	3	0.1	50	1.5	119	3.7	147	4.5
2001	17	0.7	37	1.5	90	3.7	174	7.1
2002	6	0.3	35	1.5	71	3.0	125	5.2
2003	12	0.8	50	3.2	86	5.5	107	6.9
2004	11	0.5	76	3.5	103	4.7	135	6.2
2005	12	0.6	40	1.9	114	5.5	115	5.5

Source: The Israeli Knesset Website, available at http://www.knesset.gov.il/divrey/adqform.asp
Note: percentages represent the documents containing the reference as share of the total number of online Knesset documents that year.

ascendance of Oslo (and the Rabin/Peres governments), and then returns to pre-1990 levels. Two, the Holocaust is more frequently mentioned than is anti-Semitism in general. It would be useful to know how these general trends plot alongside specific crises, and particularly useful to know whether and how frequent terms relating to victim are used during Israel's "wars of choice." In any event, the reader will have to decide whether the claim of a rising victim identity is plausible or implausible, what would count as compelling evidence one way or another, and wait for some intrepid researcher to put together the data.

While Israel arguably sees itself as a victim, the rest of the world increasingly struggles to identify with Israeli suffering. As surveyed earlier, there exist lots of possible reasons, including a world that is less sensitive to Israeli suffering because of anti-Semitism, its generation-long occupation of the captured territories, its considerable rise in political and economic power over the decades, and shifting interests of the Western powers. Yet the changing character of cosmopolitanism in general, and a rise in the cosmopolitanism of suffering in particular, deserves some credit. Cosmopolitanism is defined by principles of humanity, impartiality, and moral reciprocity, and the claim that we have obligations to help those who are in need and the greatest obligations to those in greatest need.[41] Why should the international community privilege Israeli suffering? Although the Holocaust continues to provide one justification, the universalization of the Holocaust has meant that its lessons have been extended from the Jews to all vulnerable peoples. This is not the time or the place to debate the uniqueness of the Holocaust. The fact of the matter is that the Holocaust is no longer reserved for Jews but rather has become part of the historical memory for the making of an international community. "Never again" meant not just "never again will the world stand by and allow the Jews to be killed" but rather "never again will the world stand by and do nothing in the face of genocide against any people." The universalization of the Holocaust has also been accompanied by its nationalization, which means that the "lessons" of the Holocaust are interpreted differently in different national contexts, with some emphasizing the presence of anti-Semitism and others the dangers of intolerance. Also, the internationalization and nationalization of the Holocaust has shifted its lessons from the dangers of anti-Semitism in particular to the more general danger posed by all forms of intolerance, racism, and ethnocentrism—and the heroic values of liberalism.

Israel also does not share many of the qualities of the "true victim." True victims are supposed to suffer silently, but Israel hardly passes as a silent sufferer. The true victim accepts responsibility for his fate and does not use his injuries to explain his lack of action. The true victim directly experienced the injury. Israel's association with the Holocaust, in this reading, is not direct but increasingly circumstantial. It owes not to the fact that Nazi Germany occupied and exterminated Israelis but rather to an Israel that shelters many (and is perhaps a nation of) Holocaust survivors and that claims to be the representative of the Jewish people. There is a fine line between having directly experienced the suffering and the "narcissistic appropriation of the pain of others."[42] For some, Israel is nowhere near that line, while for others it is standing on it. Israel's claim to be a victim not because of the Holocaust but rather because of attacks from Arabs and other enemies makes sense to some but not to those who insist that Israel bears responsibility for its current circumstances.[43] And, of course, Israel has had a harder time playing the victim since it became an occupying power, and each passing year has added to weight of sentiment that sees Israel not as victim but rather as perpetrator, and as a perpetrator it is partly responsible for the violence it suffers from the Palestinians.

It is worth emphasizing that the difficulty Israel faces in convincingly playing the victim on the world stage is inextricably related to the nature of cosmopolitanism in the global age. In addition to the cosmopolitanism of suffering, arguably Israel has greater difficulty exhibiting the qualities of a bona fide cosmopolitan. Israel, as a Jewish state, explicitly prioritizes the suffering of Jews, hardly the markings of a cosmopolitan. It retains an occupation over another people, thus denying them their fundamental rights. The most explosive charge, in this respect, is that Israel is becoming an "Apartheid State." The discrimination against the Arabs includes not just Palestinians who live in the occupied territories but also those Arabs who are citizens of Israel. Not only does Israel privilege the welfare and suffering of Jews over all others, but not even all Jews are created equal, for religious Jews are increasingly seen as being above and beyond (secular) law in many respects. Israel has a much more difficult time aligning itself with cosmopolitan sentiments, which, of course, is precisely why many Israeli leaders are so concerned about its legitimacy.

These changes in the character of cosmopolitanism and the Israeli political culture provide one plausible explanation for Israel's growing difficulty generating the same level of sympathy for its situation. Israel might be a victim. But so is everyone in this cosmopolitan age. Is there a reason to privilege Israeli suffering? It is not only the world that potentially feels less support for Israel. There are indications that even American Jews are losing their ability and willingness to sympathize with Israel.[44] All evidence suggests that American Jews still feel considerable anguish when Israelis are attacked on the streets of Tel Aviv, but there is also evidence that they have doubts regarding Israel's claim to be a victim for some of the same reasons that have affected much of the rest of the world. There could also be another reason: an Israel that once was central to their identity is increasingly peripheral. American Jews might soon be asking the question: why privilege the suffering of Israeli Jews?

Conclusion

Israel is certainly not the only country in the world that experiences the countervailing temptations of cosmopolitanism and particularism, but the legacy of Jewish history and the Holocaust arguably gives it a greater poign-ancy and intensity. As Robert Wistrich sympathetically writes, "The paradox of Israel being a nation of victorious conquerors and heirs of a people who barely survived a holocaust is unparalleled in any other country, and undoubtedly a source of powerful identity conflicts for many Israelis."[45] The sense of being both the conquered and the conqueror means that Israel's identity can pull powerfully in different directions, and they also can combine in unpredictable and unstable ways.

Recognizing oneself as a victim can develop into victimhood. As one observer recently wrote, "the so-called surfeit of Jewish memory is now articulated primarily as an argument about how Jewish memory exemplifies a pathological and cultural attachment to having been or being a victim."[46] The concept of victimhood is hardly a neutral way of describing a person or people. The political left are the source of most commentary (and criticism) of Israeli victimhood, and therefore can hardly be counted as unbiased source. There is no bright line to determine when an awareness of loss generates (unhealthy) perceptions about the world. And even the qualities of victimhood are disputed. But a reasonable proposition is that any people that see themselves as victims have the necessary, but not the sufficient, con-ditions for victimhood. If so, then is there any reason why Israel would be immune from such possibilities? Is Israel special also in its resistance to the charms of victimhood?

What are the signs of victimhood that observers identify in Israel?[47] To begin, Israel has a chronic sense of vulnerability that seems to persist even when structural conditions change in its favor. When Israel was a regional weakling, both economically and militarily, an obsession with vulnerability made sense. But what happens when Israel's military and economic power outstrips all its neighbors and when it has a nuclear monopoly? At what point should Israel's threat assessment change to meet the new objective structural realities? The failure to adjust, according to some observers, owes to the Jewish historical experience and the belief that virulent anti-Semitism is always possible, which, of course, makes no environment safe. Israel might have all the classic characteristics of a realist state, but it might have them in greater abundance in part because it has existed in a rougher neighborhood. Alongside a sense of vulnerability is a sense of fatalism that takes various expressions, including the "Masada Complex."[48] The Masada Complex has many meanings, but certainly one is a recurring "fantasy" that the world will surround the Jewish people and give them no choice but to commit suicide in order to deny the world its ultimate victory.

The prevailing sense of being a victim and vulnerability also translates into the related inability of Israel to recognize its own power, which has two dimensions. One is a lack of agency. To be a perpetual victim means that the world has a vendetta, which, in turn, means that there is very little one can ever do to change the situation—short of actually giving up one's beliefs (and even that might be enough for biologically inclined anti-Semites). Relatedly, there is an unwillingness to accept any criticism whatsoever, to use one's victim status as a self-defense mechanism, and even to use one's past suffering as a crutch to avoid asking tough questions about one's behavior.[49] The denial of one's power also means that it becomes difficult if not impossible to see oneself as a possible source of another's suffering. Indeed, even when Israelis recognize that their actions have caused suffering, they still manage to see themselves as the victim. At the very beginning of the peace talks with Egypt, Golda Meir reportedly said to Egyptian President Anwar Sadat: "We can forgive you for killing our sons. But we will never forgive you for making us kill yours." Israel would obviously prefer to be peaceful, but Arab hostility means that virtually any action by Israel can be justified. Two soldiers convicted of using an 11-year-old Palestinian boy as a human shield during Operation Cast Lead in Gaza wore shirts that proclaimed "We are Goldstone's Victims."[50] I have spoken with lots of Israelis who talk as if they are victims because of the practices of occupation they have delivered on the Palestinians. This denial of one's power is ironic, or perhaps inexplicable, when critics link it to another attribute of victimization: the obsessions with power and the cult of the military.[51]

These various dimensions of Israeli victimhood are nicely captured by Yossi Sarid, one of the patriarchs of the Israeli Left. Reflecting on how Israelis tend to wrap themselves in victimhood, he observed that they will insist that it is

> not the Palestinians who are victims, but we. When we kill Palestinians, build the monster wall, demolish homes and uproot plantations, we do it only for our own protection, because a nation of victims must defend themselves against those who rise to destroy it. A real psychological need is being hidden. Rituals of bereavement, the rites of mourning, and the sense of being victims, around which so much of Israeli life revolves, are deeply rooted in the national psyche. Zionism was supposed to put an end to all of this. It was supposed to turn us from a passive into an active people, from a helpless, suffering people into a nation that has taken its destiny into its own hands. On the face of it, we have succeeded. We have set up a strong state, we have immense military power, but reality has not changed our consciousness. It has remained the consciousness of a helpless, suffering people, waiting for the Cossacks to set upon us at any minute.[52]

Sarid captures all the elements of victimhood and pins them on Israel: an unhealthy attachment to one's status as a victim, a need to revel in the rituals of victimization, an inability to see how one has power to change one's situation and to harm others, the ability to use the victim label to deny one's responsibility for harm.

Israel might well be a victim, and its victimhood might be well earned, but is there a reason why the world should care about Israeli suffering more than the suffering of others?

Notes

1 David Held, *Cosmopolitanism: Ideals and Reality*, Malden, MA: Polity Press, 2010, p. 15.
2 Kwame Anthony Appiah, *Cosmopolitanism: Ethics in a World of Strangers*, New York: Norton, 2006.
3 Gerard Delanty, *The Cosmopolitan Imagination: The Renewal of Critical Social Theory*, New York: Cambridge University Press, 2009, p. 98; Luc Boltanski, *Distant Suffering*, New York: Cambridge University Press, 1999.
4 Michael Barnett, *The International Humanitarian Order*, New York: Routledge, 2010.
5 Alyson Coles, *The Cult of True Victimhood: From the War on Welfare to the War on Terror*, Stanford, CA: Stanford University Press, 2007, p. 16.
6 Ian Buruma, "The Joys and Perils of Victimhood," *New York Review of Books*, 8 April 1999.
7 Ibid.
8 Ibid.
9 Didier Fassin and Richard Rechtman, *The Empire of Trauma: An Inquiry into the Condition of Victimhood*, Princeton, NJ: Princeton University Press, 2009.
10 Coles, *The Cult of True Victimhood*, p. 5.
11 An early example is Robert Hughes, *The Culture of Complaint*, New York: Oxford University Press, 1993.
12 Tzvetan Todorov, "In Search of the Lost Crime," *New Republic*, 29 January 2001, 25 (cited in Carolyn Dean, *Aversion and Erasure: The Fate of the Victim After the Holocaust*, Ithaca, NY: Cornell University Press, 2010, p. 34).
13 Svante Lundgren, *Particularism and Universalism in Modern Jewish Thought*, Albany, NY: SUNY Press, 2001; See Lisa Leff, *Sacred Bonds of Solidarity*, Stanford, CA: Stanford University Press, 2006; Michael Miller and Scott Ury, "Cosmopolitanism: The End of Jewishness?" *European History Review*, vol. 17, no. 3, June 2010, 337–59; Natan Sznaider, "Hannah Arendt's Jewish Cosmopolitanism: Between the Universal and the Particular," *European Journal of Social Theory*, vol. 10, no. 1, 2007, 112–22; Leon Wieseltier, "Pariah and Politics: Hannah Arendt and the Jews, Part II," *New Republic*, 14 October 1981; Daniel Levy and Natan Sznaider, "The Institutionalization of Cosmopolitan Morality: The Holocaust and Human Rights," *Journal of Human Rights*, vol. 3, no. 2, June 2004, 143–57; Daniel Levy and Natan Sznaider, "Memory Unbound: The Holocaust and the Formation of Cosmopolitan Memory," *European Journal of Social Theory*, vol. 5, no. 1, 2002, 87–106; Eleonore Kofman, "Figures of the Cosmopolitan: Privileged Nations and National Outsiders," *Innovation*, vol. 18, no. 1, 2005, 83–97; Alain Finkielkraut, *The Imaginary Jew*, Lincoln: University of Nebraska Press, 1997; Svante Lundgren, *Particularism and Universalism in Modern Jewish Thought*, Binghamton, NY: Global Publications, 2001; Daniel Elazar, "Response: A Reinvented Jewish Polity in a Globalized World," in Allon Gal and Alfred Gottschalk (eds), *Beyond Survival and Philanthropy: American Jewry and Israel*, Cincinnati, OH: Hebrew Union College Press, 2000.
14 For the classic statement on Jews and universalism, see Mordechai Kaplan, *Judaism as a Civilization*, New York: Jewish Publications Society, 1934.
15 Michael Galchinsky, *Jews and Human Rights: Dancing at Three Weddings*, Lanham, MD: Rowman and Littlefield, 2007; Carole Fink, *Defending the Rights of Others: The Great Powers, the Jews, and International Minority Protection, 1878–1938*, New York: Cambridge University Press, 2006.
16 Sara Hammerschlag, *The Figural Jew: Politics and Identity in Postwar French Thought*, Chicago: University of Chicago Press, 2008.
17 Cited from David Biale, Michael Galchinsky, and Susannah Heschel, "Introduction: The Dialectic of Jewish Enlightenment," in David Biale, Michael Galchinsky,

and Susannah Heschel (eds), *Insider/Outsider: American Jews and Multiculturalism*, Berkeley: University of California Press, 1998, p. 1.

18 Daniel Levy and Natan Sznaider, *The Holocaust and Memory in the Global Age*, Philadelphia: Temple University Press, 2005, p. 48.

19 Quoted from Yosef Gorny, "Shlilat Ha-Galut: Past and Present," in Allon Gal and Alfred Gottschalk (eds), *Beyond Survival and Philanthropy: American Jewry and Israel*, Detroit, MI: Wayne State University Press, pp. 46–7.

20 Gorny, "Shlilat Ha-Galut: Past and Present," p. 46.

21 Ehud Luz, *Wrestling with an Angel: Power, Morality and Jewish Identity*, New Haven: Yale University Press, 2003. See also Arnold Eisen, *Jewish Reflection on Homelessness and Homecoming*, Bloomington, IN: Indiana University Press, 1986.

22 Although Zionist leaders might have shied away from a politics of victimhood, they were keenly sensitive to a Jewish vulnerability. See Yael Zerubavel, *Recovered Roots: Collective Memory and the Making of Israeli National Tradition*, Chicago: University of Chicago Press, 1995.

23 Idith Zertal, *Israel's Holocaust and the Politics of Nationhood*, New York: Cambridge University Press, p. 25.

24 Nachman Ben-Yehuda, *The Masada Myth: Collective Memory and Mythmaking in Israel*, Madison: University of Wisconsin, 1995, p. 74. Also see Zerubavel, *Recovered Roots*.

25 Luz, *Wrestling with an Angel*, p. 117.

26 Yael Tamir, *Liberal Nationalism*, Princeton: Princeton University Press, 1995; Luz, *Wrestling with an Angel*, p. 11; Yosef Gorny, *The State of Israel in Jewish Public Thought: The Quest for Collective Identity*, New York: New York University Press, 1994.

27 Zertal, *Israel's Holocaust and the Politics of Nationhood*, p. 3

28 Robert Wistrich, "Israel and the Holocaust Trauma," *Jewish History*, vol. 11, no. 2, Fall 1997, 13–20.

29 Martin Jaffe, "The Victim-Community in Myth and History: Holocaust, Ritual, the Question of Palestine and the Rhetoric of Christian Witness," *Journal of Ecumenical Studies*, vol. 28, Spring 1991, 230–1 (cited in Zertal, *Israel's Holocaust and the Politics of Nationhood*, p. 2).

30 Tom Segev, *The Seventh Million: The Israelis and the Holocaust*, New York: Picador, 2000. Also see Wistrich, "Israel and the Holocaust Trauma," pp. 16–17.

31 Zertal, *Israel's Holocaust and the Politics of Nationhood*, p. 95

32 Luz, *Wrestling with an Angel*, p. x.

33 Steven Rosenthal, *Irreconcilable Differences? The Waning of the American Jewish Love Affair with Israel*, Waltham, MA: Brandeis University Press, 2003.

34 Luz, *Wrestling with an Angel*, p. 10; Gorny, *The State of Israel in Jewish Public Thought*.

35 Zertal, *Israel's Holocaust and the Politics of Nationhood*, p. 111.

36 Segev, *The Seventh Million*.

37 Segev, *The Seventh Million*, p. 516 (cited from Buruma, "The Joys and Perils of Victimhood").

38 Yaron Ezrahi, *Rubber Bullets: Power and Conscience in Modern Israel*, Berkeley: University of California Press, 1998.

39 For the national differences regarding how the Holocaust has been commemorated, and especially the Americanization of the Holocaust, see Michael Bernstein, *After Tragedy and Triumph: Modern Jewish Thought and the American Experience*, New York: Cambridge University Press, 1990, chap. 3; Hilene Flanzbaum, *The Americanization of the Holocaust*, Baltimore: Johns Hopkins University Press, 1999; and Peter Novick, *The Holocaust in American Life*, New York: Mariner Books, 2000.

40 Thanks to Nadav Shelef for this suggestion and Amir Stepak for research assistance.

41 Levy and Sznaider, *Holocaust and Memory in the Global Age*.

42 Dean, *Aversion and Erasure*, p. 9.

43 Coles, *The Cult of True Victimhood*, p. 5.
44 See the recent forum in *Contemporary Jewry*, Fall 2010.
45 Wistrich, "Israel and the Holocaust Trauma," p. 17.
46 Dean, *Aversion and Erasure*, p. 32.
47 See, for instance, Juliana Ochs, "The Politics of Victimhood and Its Internal Exegetes: Terror Victims in Israel," *History and Anthropology*, vol. 17, no. 4, December 2006, 355–68.
48 Zerubavel, *Recovered Roots*, pp. 192–200.
49 Luz, *Wrestling with an Angel*, p. 226.
50 "The IDF Can't Play the Victim on Its Actions in Gaza," *Haaretz*, 10 May 2010 <http://www.haaretz.com/print-edition/opinion/the-idf-can-t-play-the-victim-on-its-actions-in-gaza-1.317236>.
51 Luz, *Wrestling with an Angel*.
52 Yossi Sarid, "Israel Does Not have a Monopoly on Suffering," *Haaretz*, 22 April 2011. Available at <http://www.haaretz.com/print-edition/opinion/israel-does-not-have-a-monopoly-on-suffering-1.357520>.

4 Israel's Dichotomous Attitude Toward International Humanitarian Law

Causes, Consequences, and Implications

Amichai Cohen and Stuart Cohen

Almost fifteen years ago, Harold Koh articulated the basic question that forms the crux of interdisciplinary research with respect to the link between international law and politics: *Why Do Nations Obey International Law?*[1] Several major scholarly schools attempt to answer this question, two of which are especially relevant to our discussion: The first is the "realist" school, which posits national interest as the almost sole determinant of compliance with international law. The second, termed the "liberal" school, focuses on societal trends and legitimacy as reasons for state compliance with international law.[2]

Israel offers an especially appropriate case for the evaluation of the efficacy of these two approaches. Partly, this is because of the seeming paradox that it represents. On the one hand, the Israeli government has frequently been accused of violating international law when acting in defense of its national security. The report of the United Nations Fact Finding Mission on the Gaza Conflict [the Goldstone Report], released in September 2009,[3] triggered just the latest in a long string of accusations on the part of international organizations to that effect. Charges of the same sort had likewise been articulated on several previous occasions, for example with reference to the Sinai Campaign (1956), the Six-Day War (1967), and the Israel Defense Forces' invasion of Lebanon in 1982. On the other hand, however, Israel has—notwithstanding its high degree of dependence on international support for its survival—managed to retain the support of major Western powers. Does "realism," the argument that political interests always take precedence over law, supply the only solution for that apparent paradox, or are other explanations viable?

What makes that question especially pertinent is the altogether exceptional degree to which Israeli courts and the Israeli executive branch have, for several years now, discussed the proper role of international law in national decision-making, especially with regard to national-security matters. This circumstance reflects Israel's lengthy application of the regime of international law of occupation to its control over the territories that Israeli forces conquered in 1967, and the willingness of the Israeli Supreme Court (ISC) to discuss legal matters deemed relevant to Israel's more recent armed conflicts with the Palestinians. Both sets of dialogues have resulted in a unique corpus of texts, the analysis of which lies at the core of our argument.

Perhaps contrary to the conventional wisdom, we shall claim that Israel has never disregarded international law. On the contrary, Israel's behavior has consistently been characterized by serious efforts to demonstrate that, even when its national security was at stake, it did, in fact, act in accordance with international law requirements. What has changed, however, is the mindset within which Israeli attitudes toward international law are framed. This chapter argues that, during the early years of statehood, Israel's expressions of respect for international law articulated an essentially *utilitarian* attempt to gain legitimacy. More recent pronouncements, by contrast, reflect two other developments. One is the growing influence within Israeli political and public life of several institutions whose respect for international law is based on their perception of the legitimacy of that corpus. Another is the increasing degree of contact maintained by members of those institutions with their colleagues overseas.

On the basis of that analysis, we shall advance a number of observations with respect to the question posed by Koh.

- For one thing, the Israeli case suggests that the reasons why nations obey international law do not remain static. In Israel's case, certainly, justifications for doing so have changed over time.
- In addition, we submit that the explanation for such changes, when they occur, cannot be restricted to changes in international law and politics. They also reflect shifts of attitudes and behavior in *domestic* decision-making institutions, shifts that are sometimes quite disconnected from international law. Hence, we argue that changes in levels of compliance with international law are heavily influenced by the emergence of mechanisms that allow international law to infiltrate the domestic system.
- Finally, we take issue with the outlook that allows Koh's question to be framed in terms of country X "obeying" international law Y. The Israeli case, we argue, indicates rather that nations frequently affect the content of international law by interpreting and applying it, especially with reference to International Humanitarian Law (IHL). In this chapter, we describe the developments in Israel's obedience to international law, especially in the area of matters relating to national security, and the application of IHL, and provide support to the above-mentioned submissions.

A historical perspective

A common assumption, shared by Israelis and non-Israelis alike, is that Israel has traditionally paid little attention to international law. Ben-Gurion's notorious (albeit elusive) reference to the United Nations as *"um shmum"* has often been cited as symptomatic of official Israeli attitudes toward international law and international public opinion in general.[4] Still more compelling evidence seems to be provided by some of the actions undertaken by Israel during Ben-Gurion's tenure as Israel's prime minister. Thus, Israel was accused of disregarding international law both when launching the 1956 Sinai Operation, which the UN subsequently condemned as a violation of the Israeli–Egyptian Armistice Agreements signed in 1949,[5] and when abducting Eichmann in 1960, an action against which Argentina lodged a legal protest, including a formal complaint to the UN Security Council.[6]

However, a closer examination of Israeli behavior during this early period, even with respect to the two specific incidents just cited, reveals a somewhat more complex picture. Israel had itself appealed to the authority of the Armistice Agreements prior to 1956. It had frequently protested their violation by Egypt during the 1950s, and had on several occasions requested UN assistance in realizing its internationally approved right to use the Suez Canal.[7]

Israel's argument that Egypt's closure of the Straits of Tiran in 1956 also violated international law was acknowledged by the UN, even though its allegedly logical corollary, that Israel was therefore entitled to resort to force, remained debatable.[8] Israeli reactions to criticisms of Eichmann's abduction conform to a similar pattern. For one thing, during the course of both the subsequent diplomatic exchanges, including the Security Council debates, Israel attempted to minimize its violation of Argentinean sovereignty, arguing that, in view of the serious crimes of genocide involved, this constituted a special case.[9] Moreover, Israel did eventually table a formal apology, thus bringing the dispute to a formal close.[10] Even so, in its decision on the Eichmann trial, handed down in Jerusalem in 1962, the ISC, far from ignoring international law, deliberately sought to interpret and apply it.[11] Indeed, that decision is still considered a model of its kind. It testifies to the ability of what was after all a very young institution (the ISC was barely 15 years old) to produce a legal opinion that is still considered a cornerstone in every international discussion of universal jurisdiction.

This duality with regard to international law reflects a deeper contradiction, embedded in Israeli society ever since the creation of the state. As Yoram Shachar and Orit Kamir have demonstrated,[12] the Declaration of Independence, Israel's constitutive charter, actually consists of two different documents—one "Jewish" (basing Israel's right to exist on historical and religious claims) and the other "democratic" (which appeals to such precedents as the Balfour Declaration, and the decision of the General Assembly of November 1947). Perhaps still more important in the present context is the duality that pervades the operative portions of the Declaration of Independence. On the one hand, the new Jewish state is to be indiscriminately open to Jewish immigration and constituted on the basis of the vision contained in traditional (Jewish) prophecies. At the same time, however, it is also to accord equal rights to all its citizens and be faithful to the principles enshrined in the UN charter.

The complexity of the views thus apparent (which, indeed, may well be internally inconsistent) provides eloquent testimony to the initial hesitations felt by early Israeli leaders with respect to international law and its role in the decision-making process. By no means can they be said to have ignored international law. They recognized its importance as a legitimizing tool. Their prism, however, was very similar to that suggested by proponents of the realist school of international law, which—incidentally or not—constituted the reigning academic paradigm in the discipline at that time.

Christian Reus-Smit defines the realist approach to international law:

> Law is fundamentally political, and in relations between states the content of international law is determined by dominant states and will not be upheld when it conflicts with their perceived political interests. It is deployed by these states for their own ends, against weaker or subordinate entities and in this respect cannot be uncoupled from politics. International law is thus not enforceable independently of the will of power states, and cannot be regarded, in any compelling sense, as binding.[13]

This view implies that international law could never limit the behavior of superpowers, nor even of reasonably strong states.[14] Nevertheless, weaker states—and, as Ben-Gurion certainly appreciated, Israel undoubtedly fit that category during its early years[15]—must employ an entirely different calculus. Whatever the intrinsic moral or ideological value that they may—or may not—attach to international law, they will always regard it as a "realistic" means of attaining national goals. Specifically, should international law reflect the wishes of one or more of the world's great powers, then any state wishing to garner their support must obey its precepts. Deviations from that rule of thumb could only be justified by especially compelling circumstances, or by an explicit exception granted by a great power. In other words, such deviations would also accord with the realist paradigm of international law.[16]

Israeli experience abounds with examples of the application of those principles. Two of the most famous instances are provided by decisions that the Israeli government reached in the immediate aftermath of the Six-Day War. The first, taken in secret on 20 June 1967, was that, in return for peace agreements with its neighbors, Israel would agree to withdraw from much of the territory recently conquered by the Israel Defense Forces (IDF).[17] Until such time, Israel would refrain from annexing any territory, other than East Jerusalem—the annexation of which was, in fact, carried out a week later with deliberate lack of fanfare.[18] The second decision was to accept UN Security Council resolution 242 (adopted unanimously on 22 November 1967), which called for the implementation of the "land for peace" formula, whereby Israel would withdraw from "territories" occupied in 1967 in exchange for peace with its neighbors.

That there were good political reasons for adopting both of those legal positions does not undermine our claim but only strengthens it. In 1967, Israel had to avoid being seen to annex territory, precisely because the default position of all states at the time was that annexation is forbidden under international law. Since world political opinion was expressed in legal terms, Israel had to speak the same language and comply with its rules. In the case of resolution 242, it may even have gained a more specific benefit by doing so.

Under the terms of the resolution, in exchange for a political concession (agreement to withdrawal from "territories"), Israel essentially received legal international recognition of its previous borders ("the Green Line") as its minimum position. Indeed, that might have been the 1967 war's most lasting achievement. By the time the International Court of Justice (ICJ) addressed this issue in 2003, during the course of its advisory opinion on the legality of the separation wall, it was taken for granted that any area west of the Green Line constitutes "Israel," and hence is not open to negotiations.[19]

Within the geo-political climate prevalent in 1967, Israel's adoption of a "realist" approach to international law was by no means unique. Long before, the "idealist" position promoted in a mood of optimism during the last year of the First World War and in its immediate aftermath by Woodrow Wilson and his European contemporaries had made way for a bleaker view. Subsequent to the Second World War, states' interest in power lay at the focus of the analysis of international relations. During the Cold War, the dominant concept was that the world was being saved from another conflagration, not by universal respect for international law, but by the threat of "mutual assured destruction." International law was mostly considered a specialized technical area, which had very little to do with actual power politics.[20] In the US, for example, even the relatively liberal scholars associated with the "New Haven School" of international law, Myres McDougal and Harold Lasswell, spoke of international law as "a process of authoritative decision-making"—a normative way of conducting politics rather than a set of norms that in practice limited the scope of state behavior.[21] Hence, the "realistic" attitudes and positions adopted by Israeli policy-makers of the period with respect to international law—attitudes that, far from pooh-poohing international law, in fact acknowledged its utility—accorded with those commonly accepted elsewhere in the Western world.

Certainly, some Israeli policy-makers were less blatant "realists" than others. Shabtai Rosene (who functioned as chief legal counsel to the Ministry of Foreign Affairs from 1948 to 1967) is known to have been sensitive to the moral virtues of international law. More notable was Moshe Sharett, Minister for Foreign Affairs between 1948 and 1956, who briefly combined the post with the office of prime minister (1954–55).

However, even in the latter case, the extent of deviation from the prevailing "utilitarian" paradigm must not be exaggerated. Detailed analysis undermines the validity of an exaggerated polarization between the approaches adopted by Sharett and Ben-Gurion.[22] Blanket depictions of Sharett as always adopting a high-minded and idealistic approach to international law, which Ben-Gurion rejected outright, likewise distort reality. Their disagreements were more over style, timing, degree, and emphasis than fundamental policy. That is why a study of Israel's conduct based on a scale ranging from respect for international law to its complete disregard would doubtless show that, even when Ben-Gurion was at the helm, it showed more consideration for international law, rather than less.

The international context

Even when realist approaches to international law and international relations were at the peak of their popularity, there always existed currents of opinion undermining the dominant view of international law as little more than a reflection of power politics. Signs of more substantive change began to appear in the 1970s. During the course of that decade, international trade law negotiations resulted in decreased tariffs and other duties by significant percentages.[23] Human rights and IHL treaties were approved and ratified, and aroused the interest of a vibrant international civil society.[24] However, these undercurrents did not find full expression until after the implosion of the Soviet bloc in 1989–90, when the world entered the era of globalization.

Considerations of space preclude a survey of the entire gamut of effects that globalization exerted on international law. The spectrum ranges from the formation of the World Trade Organization, with its extensive regulation of international economic law, to the formation of international courts and tribunals, which enforce International Humanitarian Law and International Human Rights Law.

For the purpose of the present argument, suffice it to emphasize two points:

First: Increasing numbers of scholars of international relations have since the 1990s come to accept that the rules and norms of international law (or international *regimes* as they are sometimes called in order to avoid the "L" word) possess intrinsic value and act as constraints on policy choices quite independently of traditionally "realistic" considerations.

The consensus on this point cuts across the rational/liberal scholastic divide. Thus, Robert Keohane, Joseph Nye,[25] and others—"rationalists" all— developed the argument that the reason states comply with international law is not limited to short-term calculations associated with power. They also consider long-term interests, including the ability of international law to solve problems of cooperation and collective action, and the importance of international institutions in creating stability in an increasingly complex environment. In this context, Keohane applied game theory to demonstrate that the provision of "public goods," such as free trade, would be better accomplished under an international regime.[26] Nye went on to develop the concept of "soft power."[27]

Other scholars adopted a liberal view, according to which liberal states would follow international law because of their basic commitment to the rule of law, and the "compliance pull," which international law possesses by virtue of its domestic legitimacy and appeal to ever-expanding segments of modern society.[28] For example, Anne-Marie Slaughter emphasized the importance of respect for the rule of law shown by domestic and international courts in her imagined society of liberal states, which, she hypothesized, would altogether evince considerably more consideration for international law.[29] More recently, Eyal Benvenisti has argued that the increased involvement of domestic courts in matters of national security, mainly based on claims derived from international law, is rooted in their attempt to protect core constitutional values from the growing threat posed by "the war on terror."[30]

Many of the scholars mentioned above also put forward a second claim: the increasing tendency of states to comply with international law is closely related to the diffusion of power, and of decision-making power in particular, that seems to be characteristic of the modern liberal state. Decisions as to whether to cooperate internationally or to comply with a specific international norm are not arrived at by the traditional processes associated with "the state" as a unitary sovereign actor. Much more than ever before, decision-making is now influenced—sometimes decisively so—by pressures exerted by economic interest groups, transnational networks of bureaucrats and professionals,[31] and by the rise of what Adler and Haas have famously termed transnational epistemic communities.[32]

Israel's erratic road toward a new approach to international law

Necessarily, Israel's attitudes toward international law have been affected by the idiosyncrasies of its national-security agenda. Particularly influential in this respect has been the shift in the emphasis of the IDF's operational agenda from conventional inter-state wars to "low-intensity conflicts" against asymmetric enemies, often in urban areas where conventional distinctions between combatants and noncombatants are extremely difficult to maintain.[33] Basic to the argument of this chapter, however, is the contention that developments in Israeli attitudes toward international law also run parallel to the global processes traced above, and whose influence is hardly ever acknowledged in studies of Israel's national-security behavior. More specifically, we posit two connected claims: the first, as is the case elsewhere—Israeli decision-making in the realms of foreign affairs and national security (and in other spheres too, for that matter) has become increasingly diffuse. Moreover, diffusion is not restricted to the executive. It is also evident in the extent to which other branches of government, and even non-governmental groups, participate in the decision-making process. The second—some of the institutions that have benefited from this process of diffusion, and that have hence gained more influence in the national-security realm, participate in specifically "legal" epistemic communities of a transnational nature.

Evidence of those developments can be found in several domains of Israeli public life. In the pages that follow, we shall address just three: the executive branch, the judiciary, and the non-governmental sphere.

The executive branch: from prime ministerial hegemony to "operational legal advice"

During the initial years of Israeli statehood, national-security decision-making was essentially the prerogative of the prime minister and the Minister of Defense (until 1967, both offices were for the most part held by the same person). So complete was Ben-Gurion's hegemony in this sphere that he was able to determine national-security policy almost without input from other members of his own cabinet, let alone other officials in government.[34] This was especially the case where cardinal issues were at stake. Decisions respecting Israel's participation in the Anglo-French attack on Egypt in 1956, or the development of an independent Israeli nuclear capability, were arrived at without almost any formal discussions or consultations whatsoever.[35] However, this unitary system of prime-ministerial control over national-security affairs did not last long, and perhaps could not last long. It was modified by Eshkol (even before he was forced to relinquish the Ministry of Defense late in May 1967), considerably restricted by Dayan during his heyday as Minister of Defense, and ultimately ruled out of order by later cabinets—which very much curtailed the prime minister's autonomy over decision-making with respect to such issues as the territories or Lebanon.[36]

Significantly, this diffusion of power within the executive branch was not limited to more extensive participation on the part of cabinet ministers in the decision-making process. At an operational level, other offices and officials likewise began to gain influence over decision-making. Some of the examples, such as those provided by the activities of the professional treasury establishment in the 1990s, are well known and hence require no more than brief notice.[37] More interesting, and more specifically relevant to the crux of the subject-matter of this chapter, is the development of the International Law Department (known by its Hebrew acronym DABLA) within the IDF. Hence, this particular example of decision-making diffusion will be analyzed in slightly greater depth.

As defined by General Staff orders, DABLA's role is advisory. Soldiers serving within this framework are to provide their military colleagues and superiors with advice respecting the requirements of international law.[38] In 2000, DABLA's commanding officers received permission to instrumentalize that mandate by embarking on a project known as the provision of "*operational legal advice*" (authors' emphasis). This involved supplying legal advice to officers before and during ongoing operations (and hence not just training exercises) regarding the specifics of the Laws of Armed Conflict (LOAC) or IHL.[39]

One of the distinguishing characteristics of DABLA personnel is that they simultaneously belong to two professional communities: the military and the legal profession. In this sense, their situation can be compared to that of military physicians, like whom they are prone to suffer from what sociologists term "role strain." This situation results from their attempts to meet the occasionally divergent sets of expectations of their two affiliations: as IHL lawyers and as soldiers. A superficial and perhaps intuitive view might suggest that, confronted with these dual loyalties, their priorities would be plain. The strict hierarchy and close supervision characteristic of military organizations would result in DABLA personnel acting primarily as soldiers. Only in a secondary sense would their behavior accord with the norms dictated by legal professionalism.

That impression must largely be held responsible for the fact that members of the DABLA unit—even when not entirely disregarded—have often been denigrated. Considered as little more than apologists for military actions, for which it is their task to provide legal cover, they are not thought to have any material effect on IDF decisions. We submit that such depictions distort the picture. They exaggerate the justificatory role played by DABLA lawyers, while also underplaying their *transformative* impact—the way in which they sensitize IDF commanders to international law and thereby make them more respectful of its requirements.

Several circumstances enhance DABLA's ability to fulfill a transformative function. For one thing, members of the unit are trained lawyers, and as such possess a body of knowledge not available to their military superiors. By virtue of their mastery of the law, they possess an advantage over the military commanders to whom they are attached when in the field and to whom they directly supply advice in an operational situation. As Gabriella Blum points out, final responsibility for whatever decision is ultimately taken lies with the commander.[40] That, however, might be of little solace to a commander who lacks the professional knowledge required to question the advice that his lawyer is providing.

DABLA personnel enjoy a second advantage—they are able to enlist pressure groups to support their positions. They form part of an "epistemic community" of human-rights and humanitarian lawyers.[41] They participate in conferences on international law, they write law review articles on the subject, they study with professors, and sometimes they even teach courses in one or more aspects of this discipline at universities. One consequence of this situation is a heightened awareness on their part of the price that they will have to pay if they give their approval to military policies of dubious legality. They will be criticized—perhaps even ostracized—by other members of the legal fraternity. By the same token, however, they are secure in the knowledge that—should they decide to challenge military decisions on legal grounds—they can depend upon an extensive network of legal professionals to support their point of view.

DABLA personnel are uniquely placed to exploit such advantages. Partly, this is because of the limited nature of their mandate, which relates exclusively to compliance with international law, a field in which they are considered experts. (Unlike their counterparts in the US military, DABLA lawyers are not responsible for any other area of jurisdiction.)[42] To this must be added the influence exerted on their status by the tendency of the ISC to intervene in national-security matters. Manifestations of that tendency will be addressed in greater detail below. What presently merits attention is the signal that the ISC's behavior sends to military commanders. Those who do not follow the dictates of international law (as specified by DABLA personnel) run the risk of finding their policies overruled by the ISC. In the background there lurks the real or imagined threat that international courts might apply the rule of universal jurisdiction, which creates yet another strong incentive for all commanders to seek—and accept—legal cover.

It is largely their ability to enlist external support that explains why DABLA personnel, in their capacity as legal advisors to IDF commanders in the field, exert far greater influence over Israel's national-security behavior than might perhaps be expected. Simply by virtue of its existence, the unit ensures that at the very heart of Israeli national-security decision-making apparatus lies an institution that views implementing international law as one of its major roles, and for which international law is part of its "organizational culture." Once in place, the authority thus guaranteed is deployed in a *transformative* manner and in order to change military perceptions about IHL. Advice tendered by a member of DABLA comes with a backing of very powerful external institutions. Hence, it affects not only how military commanders behave, but also how they assess behavior deemed proper.

The changing role of Israel's Supreme Court

Extensive judicial review over the formulation and implementation of policies has become perhaps the most notable characteristic of Israel's national-security decision-making process. Within that framework, especially relevant to the argument of this chapter is the extent of the involvement of the ISC in the application of International Humanitarian Law.

Justice Aharon Barak, who served as president of the ISC between 1995 and 2006, played a particularly prominent role in that development. Under his influence, from the year 2000 the Court began to hand down several decisions declaring military actions and decisions to be void, on the grounds of their incompatibility with IHL. Notable examples include the neighbor policy decision (2002; declaring illegal the IDF's use of noncombatant Palestinian neighbors and relatives to help arrest wanted suspects in the territories);[43] the cluster of Rafah decisions (2004; ordering the IDF to permit humanitarian aid to enter the Gaza Strip even during the course of an ongoing military operation);[44] the separation barrier decisions (2004, which on the basis of IHL and human-rights considerations shifted the alignment of the separation barrier in many places);[45] and the targeted killing decision (2006, allowing the use of targeted killing only if certain strict conditions are fulfilled).[46]

This enumeration of the multiplicity of instances of court intervention does not mean that the Court would necessarily involve itself in every military operation. Nevertheless, two clear conclusions emerge from the record. First, that the Court has evinced a willingness to enforce IHL on the IDF *ex ante*, that is, before an action is taken, or even while a military operation is in progress.[47] A recent statistical study shows that the Court evinces a greater willingness to intervene in matters of national security than in other topics.[48] Moreover, it seems that these interventions are especially noticeable when they touch upon issues that are of relevance to IHL (such as the separation fence or military operations). Second, and in a more subtle sense, thanks to the record of decisions taken by the Court, the "shadow" of possible judicial intervention lies over almost every military operation taken, and causes the IDF to take IHL into account.

Although the ISC might perhaps be one of the more "activist" of all national courts in this respect, its behavior is not altogether unique. National courts in many liberal democracies have shown increasing willingness to intervene in national-security matters and strike down government policies on the basis of international law. Eyal Benvenisti and George Downs have developed an elaborate theory to explain that tendency,[49] which they largely attribute to the fact that national executive branches are cooperating internationally in the "war on terror" in ways that undermine fundamental human-rights principles. Because the response to terrorism is global, traditional domestic institutions that place limits on government actions in matters of national security (such as parliaments) have little impact on the ways in which anti-terrorism campaigns are conducted. Responding to this situation, national courts began to cooperate transnationally, aiming thereby to "reclaim democracy" and protect the liberal principles that are threatened by international institutions and the war on terror.

Although Benvenisti and Downs do not explicitly rest their findings on the view that national courts constitute a "transnational network," much of their evidence does seem to point in that direction. Among other things, they direct attention to the fact that courts in various countries share an understanding of constitutional principles, to the cross citations between courts, and to the similar incentives of judges in liberal democracies.

Perhaps their study is best evaluated in light of previous work by Anne-Marie Slaughter, who made trans-judicial cooperation one of the centerpieces of her celebrated book *A New World Order*.[50] Slaughter emphasizes that national judges form part of the growing inter-governmental network. In this view, domestic courts are handing down an increasing number of decisions in which they rely on the constitutional thought of other nations, with the result that justices of Supreme Courts (or equivalent institutions) have come to constitute an especially formidable transnational network.[51] That development, of which Slaughter approves, is facilitated by two specific circumstances. One is the independence that democracies grant to the judicial system. Hence, there exist no institutional limitations on the ability of the judges to meet and exchange views with their overseas counterparts and they require no clearance from their respective foreign offices in order to meet with judges from other countries. Second, judicial decisions move easily across borders. Because court decisions, especially those of high courts, emphasize an analytical approach,[52] their logic is readily understood in other countries.

If such a transnational network or epistemic community of judges exists, some ISC justices have definitely been prominent members thereof. The previous and current president of the ISC, as well as some of that institution's leading justices, were, and still are, frequent participants in international conferences, and maintain close professional contacts with colleagues around the world. The increased reliance of the ISC on international treaties such as the Fourth Geneva Convention (1949), the additional protocol to the Geneva Conventions (1977), international human-rights treaties and decisions of international tribunals indicate that many justices of the ISC subscribe to the same values as their counterparts overseas, with whom they also share knowledge.

Professional affiliation with the transnational epistemic community of lawyers does not make justices of the ISC any less sensitive to the specific requirements of Israel's national security. If anything, quite the opposite may be the case. By virtue of that affiliation, justices of the ISC have become particularly aware of the extent to which non-Israeli courts and tribunals might intervene in matters affecting Israeli national-security decision-making, particularly sensitive to the need to respond to that intervention, and particularly well equipped to formulate an appropriate response.

All three considerations are illustrated with respect to the famous advisory opinion, which the ICJ published in 2004, declaring the separation wall to be a violation of international law. Because it viewed itself as responsible for ensuring Israel's legitimacy among the nations, the ISC felt duty bound to respond to the ICJ's advisory opinion, and did so in the *Alfei Menashe* decision that Barak authored in 2004.[53] What is interesting, however, is the form that the response took. Even though Barak disagreed with the ICJ's conclusions, he was careful not to take issue with the positions expressed in the advisory opinion any more than was absolutely necessary.[54] For national as well as professional reasons, he clearly felt it important to emphasize that, where the principles of international law are concerned, the ISC and the ICJ are in complete accord.

The non-governmental sphere

According to one count, just one Israeli NGO dealing with human rights existed prior to the outbreak of the first *intifada* in December 1987. By 2002, when the second *intifada* was at its height, the number had grown to 26 and a vibrant NGO "community" had been formed.[55]

Israeli human-rights NGOs were never an important force in Israeli politics. They were far too small to pose an electoral challenge and could hardly claim to be located at the heart of the public consensus. In fact, mainstream Israeli politicians and public opinion treated them as potential traitors, who promoted the rights of Palestinian terrorists and their supporters over the right of Israelis to security. Nevertheless, NGOs and INGOs have been able to exert a vastly disproportionate influence on Israeli national-security decision-making, and claim much of the credit for the way in which that process has adopted a more respectful approach toward international law.

Part of that success must be attributed to the fact that Israeli human-rights activists do not operate in isolation. Rather, they constitute part of a global network, which operates at multiple levels. Often, their contacts with international NGOs and even foreign governments can be traced back to the "initiation" stages of an individual's involvement in human-rights issues. Many of the persons who formed NGOs in Israel had previously studied abroad, frequently with the help of grants funded by international organizations and NGOs.[56]

Once established, many NGOs receive corporate financial support from international NGOs (such as the New Israel Fund), foundations (e.g., the Ford Foundation), and foreign governments (European governments are especially active in supporting Israeli NGOs).[57] At an operational level, moreover, Israeli NGOs coordinate their campaigns to change Israel's policies with International NGOs, international organizations, and the UN.[58]

Significantly, those campaigns do not take the form of attempts to exert conventional political pressure—an approach which, considering the unpopularity of Israeli NGOs, would, if adopted, doubtless have been doomed to failure. Rather, working in conjunction with their overseas colleagues, Israeli human-rights activists have sought to influence Israel's national-security policies by presenting petitions to the ISC based on principles of international law. This has proved to be an especially effective method, not least because it takes advantage of the sensitivity that the ISC (as shown above) is in any case evincing toward alleged international law violations. Petitions, therefore, serve the interests of both sides of the equation. They promise to supply NGOs with a much more influential audience than their numerical inferiority would otherwise have allowed. At the same time, they allow justices of the Supreme Court to hand down decisions on subjects that might otherwise not have been formally submitted for their professional review.

The so-called targeted killing case[59] offers a fine example of this convergence of interests. Because DABLA was also involved in this case, it also demonstrates the process of diffusion that characterizes the process of Israeli national-security decision-making at large.

As originally conceived by IDF commanders, targeted killings offered a solution to an operational-military dilemma born of the control exercised by the Palestinian authority over territories from which terrorists operated. With the outbreak of the second *intifada* in 2000, it became obvious that Palestinian security officials would not arrest even identified terrorists; however, IDF forces could not do so either. "Targeted killings" (i.e., the killing of individually selected persons not in Israeli custody) thus seemed to be the only way of eliminating the threat that they posed to the lives of Israel's citizens.

It is a significant sign of the prevailing atmosphere that by the turn of the new millennium IDF commanders thought it necessary, or prudent, to ask DABLA for an opinion on the legality of this mode of operation. The response was positive—but guardedly so. DABLA's legal assumption was that the outbreak of the second *intifada* had brought into being a non-international armed conflict between Israel and Palestinian organizations, a situation for which the relevant norms are the international laws of non-international armed conflict. On the one hand, therefore, DABLA's opinion designated terrorists as "illegal combatants," and hence as persons not protected by the terms of the Geneva Conventions and protocols. For that reason, they constituted legitimate targets. On the other hand, however, the opinion made its license to kill conditional on the fulfillment of a number of strict limitations, made especially necessary by the risk that the proximity of innocent bystanders to the targeted terrorist could result in the loss of civilian lives ("collateral damage"). Specifically, DABLA stipulated that the IDF has to pay attention to the principle of proportionality—which limits the possibilities of use of force when civilians may be hurt. Soon enough, the IDF translated that requirement to mean that a military lawyer had to be present for every approval of targeted killing operations.[60]

Considering these provisos to be inadequate, NGOs swiftly petitioned the ISC. Targeted killings, they claimed, would, under domestic Israeli law, obviously be considered murder; hence, the military should be forbidden from resorting to them. This argument clearly did not meet with the approval of Chief Justice Barak, who presided over the case, and he soon instructed the petitioners to rewrite their petition, this time basing themselves on international law.[61] To that end, the NGOs enlisted the help, as an "expert witness," of Antonio Cassese, a famous international law scholar, and a former judge at the International Criminal Tribunal for Former Yugoslavia. Cassese duly wrote an opinion, which concluded that targeted killings do violate the laws of war, unless the terrorist is specifically engaged in concrete military action (like shooting) when he is targeted. The case then went back to the ISC.

As an attempt to navigate a passage through a legal minefield, Barak's judgment in the targeted killing case deserves to be considered a judicial *tour de force*. It articulated his sensitivity to the needs of Israel's national security. At the same time, it also reflects a clear decision on Barak's part to relate to Cassese's opinion, which there were good reasons to consider was shared by several other members of international tribunals—and hence by much of the epistemic legal community to which Barak himself belonged.

In summarizing his judgment, Barak conceded that "we cannot determine that a preventive strike is always legal, just as we cannot determine that it is always illegal. All depends on the question whether the standards of customary international law of armed conflict allows this preventive strike or not."[62] On that basis, Barak interprets specific articles in the first additional protocol to the Geneva Conventions (1977) and concludes that in some cases terrorists, even though they are not soldiers, constitute legitimate targets in an armed conflict because they "directly participate" in hostilities, and hence lose their protected status as civilians.[63] More important to Barak are the protection of innocent civilians, and the application of the principle of proportionality of the damage to the uninvolved. Barak lays down specific requirements that the IDF has to fulfill before approving a targeted killing operation, in order to minimize collateral casualties. In addition, Barak required the military to open an investigation into any operation during the course of which a civilian life had been lost.[64]

Barak's decision, we submit, cannot be seen in isolation. It is not merely an interpretation of international law by a domestic court. Rather, it is a step in a long process of dialogue between institutions implementing international law. In order to understand this point, a wider view of the issue of targeted killing is required.

An important background to the decision of the ISC is the extended use of *universal jurisdiction* by foreign courts. Universal jurisdiction is "criminal jurisdiction based solely on the nature of the crime, without regard to where the crime was committed, the nationality of the alleged or convicted perpetrator, the nationality of the victim, or any other connection to the state exercising such jurisdiction."[65] An important principle in the application of universal jurisdiction is the principle of complementarity. In most countries, universal jurisdiction is not used if the country in which the alleged crime occurred investigated and prosecuted the suspects itself.[66]

This creates an interesting dialogue between national courts.[67] Barak was certainly aware that a decision to provide a blanket approval to any targeted killing operation might open the door to foreign court intervention, under the theory that, absent an Israeli investigation, the *universal jurisdiction* doctrine applies. Barak's decision, ordering the opening of an Israeli investigation into alleged violation of IHL, was intended to avoid precisely that result.

Barak's strategy seems to have worked exactly as he intended. Pursuant to Barak's judgment, NGOs renewed their petition for an independent investigation of the targeted killing of Saleh Shehadeh in 2003, when the operation mounted against Shehadeh, a terrorist responsible for the death of numerous Israelis, resulted in the additional death of 14 noncombatants, members of Shehadeh's family and neighbors. Under the terms of universal jurisdiction, charges were presented by NGOs in several European courts against senior Israeli officers, who were accused of committing war crimes by disregarding the lives of innocent civilians. Confronted with this challenge, which also of course presented a threat to the professional standing of Israeli justices in the transnational legal community, Barak demanded that the IDF open an independent investigation into the Shehadeh operation.[68] In at least one respect, his maneuver was successful. Apprised that an independent military investigation was to take place, the Spanish court decided not to apply the principle of universal jurisdiction in this case.[69]

As shown by the Shehadeh example, the power of the ISC was buttressed by the potential use of universal jurisdiction by the Spanish court. Because of the potential use of universal jurisdiction, the ISC could *domestically* present the use of international law as an unavoidable move, intended to block universal jurisdiction over cases. Hence, the position of the ISC to require implementation of international law was strengthened by an external institution, which is part of the same epistemic community of judges.

The targeted killings case at the ISC is also important because of its after-effects on international law. Targeted killings are used by other countries as well. Especially prominent is the use of this method by the US military. However, the decision of the ISC was the first ever judicial pronouncement on the legality of this method. As such, the decision of the ISC also had a *formative* effect on international law. It provoked responses from many international scholars. Most importantly, it was an important trigger to the issuance of an important "soft law" instrument—the *ICRC Interpretative Guidance on the Notion of Direct Participation in Hostilities.*[70] While the ICRC document does not fully adopt the position of the ISC, it certainly accepts its basic premise, namely that terrorists may be considered as civilians directly participating in hostilities, and hence forming a legitimate target.

Conclusions

Self-evidently, an enormous gulf separates reactions to the Shehadeh case from the attitude toward international law that prevailed during Israel's first decades. Many of the differences reflect the massive shifts that have occurred in the military environment within which Israeli forces operate, and especially the increasing prominence of "low-intensity conflicts" (often in heavily popu-lated urban environments) on the IDF's campaign record. We suggest, however, that additional processes have also been at work.

What has changed is not merely the context of national-security policy-making and implementation, but—in a more profound sense—its form and substance. For one thing, the "actors" now involved in those processes have become more numerous and more varied, thereby exposing national-security dialogues to a far wider spectrum of influences and pressures than was once the case. Second, considerations rooted in principles of international law—which, although always of relevance to Israel's national-security thinking, were traditionally assessed in essentially utilitarian terms—have in recent years come to be vested, at least in some influential circles, with the status of moral imperatives. From their perspective, international law is not merely a tool that can facilitate the attainment of national goals. Rather, it articulates a set of norms that have to be observed because of their intrinsic value.

These changes have not merely developed simultaneously. As has been seen, they are also in many respects the results of interaction between the formal and sustentative dimensions of the national-security framework. Precisely for that reason, however, their impact on Israel's national-security behavior has not been uniform. As the Shehadeh case demonstrates, Israel, like many other countries, is becoming a more complex entity, in which it is no longer possible to decide with any certainty that "the state" is violating or complying with international law.

Certain Israeli institutions comply with international law, others violate it, and still others try to affect the level of compliance. Undoubtedly, in many cases, the end result is that the specific action taken is *not* in compliance with international law. What can be said, however, is that—increasingly—growing sectors of both official and public society are taking international law into account when assessing national-security options. Therein, perhaps, lies the greatest importance of the contribution of DABLA, of the Supreme Court, and of NGOs to this area. All constitute components within the transnational epistemic communities that have promoted the dissemination of international law worldwide. However, precisely because of that status, all have also played a significant role in shaping the domestic Israeli atmosphere. In different ways, and with varying degrees of success, all have become participants in the project that Harold Koh termed "internalization"—the import of international law not merely into the legal system, but rather into the social and political fabric of society at large.[71]

In summary, we posit that the Israeli case teaches two important lessons about the process of internalization.

- The first, and most prominent, is that the process resembles a chain reaction. The development of NGOs meant that many more cases would be brought to the ISC. Development of international institutions allowed the ISC to require more compliance with international law by domestic institutions. Pressure exerted by the ISC caused the IDF to pay more attention to IHL, and as a result the position of DABLA was strengthened. These emerging institutions enforced and supported each other on the process of internalization of international law.
- Second, because international law is increasingly framed in open-ended and ambiguous terms, and deals with ever-developing new areas, it requires interpretation. Hence, the process of internalization is also one of interpretation, which in turn affects the contents of international law. In this sense, at least, international law may be intrinsically democratic, in the sense that each state has a "voice" in its creation and development. This observation offers another caveat to the "realist" perspective, according to which the only reason that small states comply with international law is their need to gain and retain the support of stronger powers. In fact, the contemporary decentralized formation of international law also allows small states to be part of its creation. For Israel, this is the upside of the process. The downside, of course, is that other countries and institutions opposing Israel may also try to interpret international law according to their interests, as might have been the case in the Goldstone Report. Whether, overall, Israel stands to gain or lose from this process still remains to be seen.

Notes

1 Harold H. Koh, "Why Do Nations Obey International Law?" *Yale Law Journal,* vol. 106, no. 8, 1997, 2599–659; "Bringing International Law Home," *Houston Law Review,* vol. 35, 1998, 623–82.
2 For a recent survey of theories of compliance with international law, see Beth A. Simmons, *Mobilizing for Human Rights: International Law in Domestic Politics,* New York: Cambridge University Press, 2009.
3 Available at UN Human Rights Council, <http://www2.ohchr.org/english/bodies/hrcouncil/specialsession/9/FactFindingMission.htm>.
4 Michael Brecher, *The Foreign Policy System of Israel: Setting, Images, Process,* London: Oxford University Press, pp. 336ff; Aaron S. Klieman, *Israel and the World After Forty Years,* Washington, DC: Pergamon, 1990, p. 4. As Neil Kaplan has shown, the only primary evidence for Ben-Gurion's use of this phrase is an entry in Moshe Sharett's personal diary dated 29 March 1955. Neil Kaplan, "'Oom-Shmoom' Revisited: Israeli Attitudes towards the UN and the Great Powers, 1948–1960," in

Abraham Ben-Zvi and Aaron Klieman (eds), *Global Politics: Essays in Honour of David Vital*, London: Cass, 2001, p. 169.

5 UNGA Resolution 997 (ES-I) (2 November 1956).

6 UNSC Resolution 138 (1960).

7 UNSC Resolution 95 (1 September 1951); Israel's claim was based on the *Constantinople Convention Respecting the Free Navigation of the Suez Maritime Canal* (1888), which stipulated that the canal would remain open in war and in peace.

8 On the rights of navigation in the Gulf of Aqaba, see Leo Gross, "Passage Through the Straits of Tiran and the Gulf of Aqaba," *Law and Contemporary Problems*, vol. 3, 1968, 125–46.

9 UNSC Resolution 138 (1960).

10 For an extended review of these discussions, see Matthew Lippman, "The Trial of Adolf Eichmann and the Protection of Human Rights under International Law," *Houston Journal of International Law*, vol. 5, no. 1, 1982, 1–34, especially pp. 7–11.

11 CA 336/61 Eichmann v. Attorney General PD 16, 2037 (1962). Available in English at <http://www.ess.uwe.ac.uk/genocide/Eichmann_Index.htm>.

12 O. Kamir, "The Declaration has Two Faces: The Interesting Story of the 'Zionist Declaration of Independence' and the 'Democratic Declaration of Independence'," *Iyuney Mishpat*, vol. 23, 2000, 473–538; Y. Shachar, "The Early Drafts of the Declaration of Independence of the state of Israel," *Iyuney Mishpat*, vol. 26, 2002, 523–600 [both in Hebrew].

13 Christian Reus-Smit, "The Politics of International Law," in Christian Reus-Smit (ed.), *The Politics of International Law*, Cambridge, UK: Cambridge University Press, 2004, p. 15.

14 Jerome Frank bluntly makes this point, in a famous letter to Felix Cohen:

> My basic point is that the so-called principles of international law are applied, or not applied, in particular instances, in accordance with what a particular country considers, at the particular moment, to be for the welfare of its citizens. Consequently, any given so-called principle of international law is often applied by any given country to one set of facts in one part of the world and not applied to what might seem to be a similar set of facts in another part of the world. Not to recognize that such is the manner in which so-called international law is always applied is to ignore the facts of life.

Posted by Dan Ernst on "Legal History Blog", <http://legalhistoryblog.blogspot.com/2008/06/legal-realism-and-international-law.html>.

15 "We are dependent on the whole world like every country – and more so than every other country," diary entry, 22 July 1950, quoted in Uri Bialer, "Facts and Pacts: Ben-Gurion and Israel's International Orientation, 1948–1956," in Ronald Zweig (ed.), *David Ben-Gurion: Politics and Leadership in Israel*, London: Cass, 1991, pp. 216–17.

16 In their neo-realist analysis of Customary International Law, Goldsmith and Posner suggest that most cases of apparent "compliance" with international law are either when a state's interests coincide with international law, or when strong states compel weaker states to follow it. Jack L. Goldsmith and Eric Posner, *The Limits of International Law*, Oxford, UK: Oxford University Press, 2005, pp. 23–44.

17 Tom Segev, *1967—Israel, the War, and the Year that Transformed the Middle East*, New York: Metropolitan Books, 2007, pp. 500–60.

18 On 27 June 1967, the government rushed through the Knesset all three readings of a bill to amend the Law and Government Ordinance of 1948 so that the executive could delineate the borders of the State of Israel. Armed with that power, on the grant of which only representatives of the Communist parties passed more than perfunctory comment, the same day the Ministry of the Interior publicized the precise

geographical coordinates of the border amendments that it was making. Anybody with a map to hand could, of course, immediately discover that East Jerusalem had thus been incorporated into Israel. However, nowhere in either the Knesset legislation or the government decree was the city expressly named. Gershom Gorenberg, *The Accidental Empire: Israel and the Birth of Settlements, 1967–1977*, New York: Times Books, 2006, pp. 42–64.

19 Advisory Opinion: Legal Consequences of the Construction of a Wall in the Occupied Palestinian Territories (ICJ, 2004) 43 ILM 1009 (9 July 2004) para. 101.
20 For a general description, see Koh, "Why Do Nations Obey International Law?" pp. 2615–18.
21 Rosalyn Higgins, *Problems and Process: International Law and How We Use It*, Oxford, UK: Oxford University Press, 1994, p. 267.
22 Kaplan, "'Oom-Shmoom' Revisited," pp. 167–99.
23 Koh, "Why Do Nations Obey International Law?"
24 Simmons, *Mobilizing for Human Rights*, pp. 42–56.
25 E.g., Robert O. Keohane and Joseph S. Nye, *Power and Interdependence: World Politics in Transition*, Boston: Little Brown, 1977.
26 Robert O. Keohane, *After Hegemony*, Princeton, NJ: Princeton University Press, 1984.
27 Joseph S. Nye, *Soft Power: The Means to Success in World Politics*, New York: Public Affairs, 2004.
28 Thomas Franck, *The Power of Legitimacy Among Nations*, New York: Oxford University Press, 1990.
29 Anne-Marie Slaughter, "International Law in a World of Liberal States," *European Journal of International Law*, vol. 6, no. 1, 1995, 503–38.
30 Eyal Benvenisti, "Reclaiming Democracy: The Strategic Uses of Foreign and International Law by National Courts," *American Journal of International Law*, vol. 102, no. 2, 2008, 241–74.
31 Anne-Marie Slaughter, "Government Networks: The Heart of the Liberal Democratic Order," in Gregory H. Fox and Brad R. Roth (eds), *Democratic Governance and International Law*, Cambridge, UK: Cambridge University Press, 2000, pp. 199–235; "Agencies on the Loose? Holding Government Networks Accountable," in George Berman, Matthias Herdegen, and Peter Lindseth (eds), *Transatlantic Regulatory Cooperation: Legal Problems and Political Prospects,* Cambridge, UK: Cambridge University Press, 2000, pp. 521–46; "Global Government Networks, Global Information Agencies, and Disaggregated Democracy," *Michigan Journal of International Law*, vol. 24, 2003, 1041–75.
32 Emanuel Adler, "The Emergence of Cooperation: National Epistemic Communities and the International Evolution of the Idea of Nuclear Arms Control," *International Organization*, vol. 46, no. 1, 1992, 101–45; Emanuel Adler and Peter M. Haas, "Conclusion: Epistemic Communities, World Order, and the Creation of a Reflective Research Program," *International Organization*, vol. 46, no. 1, 1992, 367–90; Peter M. Haas, "Epistemic Communities and International Policy Coordination," *International Organization,* vol. 46, no. 1, 1992, 1–35; and "Do Regimes Matter? Epistemic Communities and Mediterranean Pollution," *International Organization*, vol. 43, no. 3, 1989, 377–403.
33 Stuart Cohen, *Israel and Its Army: From Cohesion to Confusion*, London: Routledge, 2009, esp. chap. 3, "The Changing Operational Landscape," pp. 35–52.
34 Yehuda Ben-Meir, *Civil-Military Relations in Israel*, New York: Columbia University Press, 1995, p. 144.
35 On the decision to go to war in 1956, see Motti Golani, "Shall We Go to War? and If We Do, When? The Genesis of the Internal Debate in Israel on the Road to the Sinai War," *Israel Affairs*, vol. 6, no. 3, 2000, 22–42, esp. pp. 26, 30, 33. On the nuclear program: "Ben-Gurion [sic] did not obtain a cabinet decision on the secret project he had initiated, and he did not allow the issue to be debated in the

military," Avner Cohen, *Israel and the Bomb*, New York: Columbia University Press, 1998, p. 71.

36 Ben-Meir, *Civil-Military Relations in Israel*, p. 151.

37 Examples are provided by the way in which Treasury officials promoted such wide-ranging international policy initiatives as Israel's free trade agreements with the EU (1995–2000) and its application for membership of the World Trade Organization (1995). Both economic decisions had wide-ranging effects on domestic Israeli policies, and both were effectively taken by unelected officials.

38 On the official definition of the role of military lawyers, see Directive of Supreme Command (DSC) 2.0613 sections 9, 10. On the advisory role of the military lawyer, see Protocol of the testimony of Brig. General Avichai Mandelblit, the Chief MAG, before the Winograd commission, 16 January 2007 [Hebrew].

39 Some authors, especially in the US, use these as synonyms. Traditionally, the laws of war were called the Laws of Armed Conflict. This signifies their general goal— to regulate armed conflicts according to pre-agreed forms. During the second half of the twentieth century, the terms were changed and the nomenclature applied to this area of law became International Humanitarian Law. This change also shifted the focus of legal attention from agreements between armies about military conduct to the protection of civilians.

40 Gabriella Blum, "The Role of the Client: The President's Role in Government Lawyering," *Boston College International and Comparative Law Review*, vol. 32, no. 2, 2009, 275–87.

41 Ariel Kolonomos, "Tying the Gordian Knot: Targeted Killings and the Ethics of Prevention" (paper presented at a conference on "The Moral Dimension of Asymmetrical Warfare" organized by The Netherlands Defense Academy in Amsterdam, 4 October 2006).

42 For a description of "military lawyering" in the US armed forces, see Laura A. Dickinson, "Military Lawyers on the Battlefield: An Empirical Account of International Law Compliance," *American Journal of International Law*, vol. 104, no. 1, 2010, 1–28.

43 The relevant ISC decisions of the period are reviewed in: Amichai Cohen and Stuart Cohen, *Israel's National Security Law: Political Development and Historical Dynamics*, London: Routledge, 2011, pp. 143–73.

44 ISC, 4764/04, *Physicians for Human Rights v. IDF Commander of Gaza* 58(5) PD 385 (2004) ("Rafah Operation" case). Available in English at <http://elyon1.court. gov.il/files_eng/04/640/047/a03/04047640.a03.htm>.

45 ISC, 2056/04, *Beit Sourik Village Council v. Government of Israel* 58(5) PD 807 (2003); 43 ILM, 1099 (2004) ("Separation Barrier" case). Available in English at <http://elyon1.court.gov.il/files_eng/04/560/020/A28/04020560.a28.htm>.

46 ISC, 769/02, *Public Committee against Torture in Israel v. Government of Israel* (Judgment) 14 December 2006 ("Targeted Killing" case). Available in English at <http://elyon1.court.gov.il/files_eng/02/690/007/a34/02007690.a34.pdf>.

47 The ISC, sitting as the high court of justice, is perhaps the most flexible court in the world in terms of accepting appeals. It actually has no "standing" limitation, and very rarely resorts to such avoidance doctrines as categorizing a particular subject as a "political question" or related to "foreign affairs." Furthermore, access to the ISC in appeals emanating from the territories is even easier. The unique location of the Palestinian–Israeli conflict, which is taking place very close to Israel's population centers, the large number of NGOs dispersed all over the territories, the flexibility of the ISC, which allows almost direct access to Supreme Court justices around the clock—all result in a span of opportunities almost unimaginable in other Western democracies, to say nothing of non-democratic regimes.

48 Menachem Hofnung and Karen Wienshall Margel, "Judicial Setbacks, Material Gains: Terror Litigation and the Israeli High Court of Justice," Unpublished

Manuscript, on file with authors. We thank Professors Hofnung and Wienshall Margel for generously acquainting us with their research.

49 See, e.g., Benvenisti, "Reclaiming Democracy," pp. 241–74; Eyal Benvenisti and George Downs, "Toward Global Checks and Balances," *Constitutional Political Economy*, vol. 20, no. 3, 2009, 366–87; "National Courts, Domestic Democracy, and the Evolution of International Law," *European Journal of International Law*, vol. 20, no. 1, 2009, 59–72.

50 Anne-Marie Slaughter, *A New World Order*, Princeton, NJ: PUP, 2004.

51 Ibid., p. 65.

52 Ibid., p. 77.

53 ISC, 7957/04, *Mara'abe v. Prime Minister of Israel* (2006). Available in English at <http://elyon1.court.gov.il/files_eng/04/570/079/A14/04079570.a14.htm>.

54 E.g., regarding settlements, the ICJ simply declared that the settlements were illegal, and therefore their protection was not a legitimate reason for determining the route of the separation barrier. The ISC concluded that, even if the settlements were illegal (and it was careful not to adjudicate this matter), this does not mean that the settlers lost their right to life, and their protection continues to be a legitimate consideration.

55 Nitza Berkovitz and Neve Gordon, "The Political Economy of Transnational Regimes: The Case of Human Rights," *International Studies Quarterly*, vol. 52, no. 4, 2008, 881–904. In part, that development reflected the growing sensitivity in Israeli society at large to human-rights issues. But it also owed much to the two *intifadas*, which helped to thrust Palestinian rights to the top of the Israeli political agenda, and to Israel's ratification of several important Human Rights Conventions in 1992, which induced INGOs and NGOs to monitor Israel's compliance with those documents.

56 One such program is the Israel–US Civil Liberties Program at American University, Washington College of Law. Each year, two Israeli human-rights lawyers participate in an LLM program at AU. Their studies are funded by the New Israel Fund, and they usually specialize in international law. Upon returning to Israel, some of the graduates of the program have formed new NGOs or have become leading figures in existing ones (e.g., Dan Yakir is now Chief Legal Counsel of IACR, and Yousef Jabareen founded *Adallah*—the leading Arab NGO).

57 Berkovitz and Gordon, "The Political Economy of Transnational Regimes."

58 Israeli NGOs make a noticeable attempt to distance themselves from such cooperation, when possible. For example, when Israeli NGOs were accused of cooperating with the Goldstone Report, they were quick to respond by distancing themselves. When Israeli NGOs published ads supporting an independent investigation into Israel's actions in *Operation Cast Lead*, the only NGOs that signed the ad were Israeli. Of course, in view of the accusations against Israeli NGOs as being conspirators against Israel, this position is understandable.

59 ISC, 769/02, *Public Committee against Torture in Israel v. Government of Israel* (note 46 above).

60 Daniel Resiner, former head of the ILD (1995–2004), quoted by Alan Craig, "Lebanon 2006 and the Front of Legitimacy," *Israel Affairs*, vol. 15, no. 4, 2009, 427–44. On the principle of proportionality in armed conflicts, see Judith G. Gardam, "Proportionality and Force in International Law," *American Journal of International Law*, vol. 87, no. 3, 1993, 391–413.

61 ISC, 769/02, *Public Committee against Torture in Israel v. Government of Israel*— interim decision 18 April 2002.

62 ISC, 769/02, *Public Committee against Torture in Israel v. Government of Israel*— judgment (note 46 above).

63 Barak's decision is based on the wording of the first additional protocol to the Geneva Conventions, which states in article 51(3): "Civilians shall enjoy the

protection afforded by this section, unless and for such time as they take a direct part in hostilities." *Protocol Additional to the Geneva Conventions of 12 August 1949, and Relating to the Protection of Victims of International Armed Conflicts* [Protocol I], 8 June 1977, 1125 U.N.T.S. 3., art. 51(3).
64 See, generally, Amichai Cohen and Yuval Shany, "A Development of Modest Proportions: The Application of the Principle of Proportionality in the *Targeted Killing* Case," *Journal of International Criminal Justice*, vol. 5, no. 2, 2007, 310–21.
65 See Stephen Macedo (ed.), *The Princeton Principles on Universal Jurisdiction*, 2001. Available at <http://lapa.princeton.edu/hosteddocs/unive_jur.pdf>, hereinafter, the Princeton Principles.
66 E.g., *Institut de Droit International*, Resolution on Universal Criminal Jurisdiction with regard to the Crime of Genocide, Crimes Against Humanity and War Crimes (Krakow Session, 2005). Available at <http://www.idi-iil.org/idiE/resolutionsE/2005_kra_03_en.pdf>.
67 Amichai Cohen, "Domestic Courts and Sovereignty," in Tomer Broude and Yuval Shany (eds), *The Shifting Allocation of Authority in International Law*, Oxford: Hart, 2008, pp. 265–92.
68 ISC, 8794/03 *Hass v. Chief Military Advocate General* (2008).
69 Ido Rosenzweig and Yuval Shany, "Update on Universal Jurisdiction: Spanish Court of Appeals Decides to Close the Inquiry into the Targeted Killing of Salah Shehadeh," 17 July 2009. Available at <http://www.idi.org.il/sites/english/ResearchAndPrograms/NationalSecurityandDemocracy/Terrorism_and_Democracy/Newsletters/Pages/8th%20Newsletter/4/Shehadeh.aspx>.
70 *Interpretative Guidance on the Notion of Direct Participation in Hostilities* (ICRC, Geneva, 2009). Available at <http://www.icrc.org/eng/resources/documents/article/review/review-872-p991.htm>.
71 Koh, "Why Do Nations Obey International Law?" p. 2653.

5 Israel and the World

The Democracy Factor

Naomi Chazan

At precisely the same time that democratically driven upheavals are spreading throughout the Arab world, Israel is in the midst of a democratic recession. This process has widespread implications not only for its international position, but also for its internal priorities and its very identity.

The debate over Israel's global standing is as old as the state itself. For over six decades, two schools of thought have vied with each other: that which claims that, regardless of what it does, Israel stands alone in a hostile world; and that which argues that Israel's actions can—and do—affect its position in the international arena.[1] Although these approaches reflect different conceptions, values, norms, and perceptions of Israel and its nature, they have always been an integral part of Israel's democratic discourse.

Recently, however, this discussion has taken on an innovative twist: Israel's growing isolation has become a topic of intense domestic controversy with broad implications for its democratic character and, by extension, for its global positioning. The question of Israel's place in the world has been inter-nalized, becoming a major cause for anti-democratic trends; the enemy from outside is now being hunted at home, leading to a democratic recession that further marginalizes Israel in the world. The civic nature of Israeli identity, as defined by its founders, is being questioned by a growing neo-nationalist surge bent on displacing the universal and Jewish values of equality, justice, and tolerance embedded in its Declaration of Independence with an ethnically driven mindset that ties the connection between the land and the people to an exclusivist agenda which denies diversity and denigrates pluralism. A process of de-democratization has been set in motion, dividing not only Israelis, but also increasingly splitting the Jewish world. Its consequences distance Israel even further from its democratic allies.

Why is this process taking place? What are its key characteristics? Who is fuelling the campaign and for what purpose? What are the results? And what does the systematic attempt to constrain Israel's democracy mean not only for its relationship with the outside world, but also for its own being? This chapter seeks to answer these questions by tracing recent anti-democratic cam-paigns in Israel, examining their sources, analyzing responses, and assessing their implications.

The main contention of this analysis is that systematic efforts to delegitimize, de-fund, and ultimately destroy alternative groups and viewpoints in Israel are contributing directly to undermining the foundations of Israel's democracy and, by extension, the basis for its international legitimacy. Israel's struggle to sustain a democratic order has always been its best defense; the erosion of this commitment weakens its internal fabric as well as its international viability. From this perspective, the determination of Israel's own identity lies, first and foremost, in its own hands.

De-democratization: The dynamics

The groundwork for the limitation of democratic diversity in Israel under the guise of nationalist purity has been in the making for quite some time, gathering momentum during the past decade, in the wake of the collapse of the Oslo process and the outbreak of the second *intifada*. Retreat from the belief in the attainability of a workable peace with the Palestinians during the past decade has been accompanied by the systematic marginalization of the peace camp in the country.[2] This process has come together with the nurturing of a climate of suspicion toward the Arab citizens of Israel, their elected leaders, and their key civic organizations.[3] These anti-Arab sentiments were particularly evident during the 2009 elections, with several parties (most notably Israel Beiteinu headed by Avigdor Lieberman) placing the demand for loyalty to the state as a precondition for citizenship at the forefront of their campaign. These calls have been buttressed by persistent attacks on the court system in particular and the rule of law in general.

The outright victory of right-wing parties at the polls in February 2009 immediately following the Israeli operation in Gaza provided the backdrop for a far more intense and deliberate assault on progressive groups and opinions in the country. These systematic, orchestrated, and exceedingly well-planned efforts gathered momentum and not inconsiderable traction during the ensuing three years.

The symptoms of stepped-up processes of de-democratization follow a pattern familiar from historical and comparative experiences elsewhere. Self-styled patriotic groups have targeted growing segments of Israeli society, labeling them as misguided and casting doubts on their loyalty.

The first and primary focus of this campaign has been progressive (Jewish and Arab) civil society in Israel. Israeli civil institutions, which have blossomed during the past three decades as a result of both economic decentralization and as a reflection of societal diversification, have played a prominent role in initiating social change in the country. They have also been a central force in democratizing Israeli society through expanding the parameters of public discourse, enhancing civil liberties, protecting minority rights, promoting agreement on the rules of the game, inculcating non-violent norms of citizen action, and championing a diversity of voices and opinion.

The initial signs of a broad offensive against these institutions surfaced in September 2009, with the release of a major study on foreign government funding of Israeli civil society groups by two organizations, NGO Monitor (a self-appointed civil society watchdog) and the Institute for Zionist Strategies (IZS) (a think-and-do tank associated with right-wing worldviews).[4] This report was then used as the centerpiece of a conference held at the Knesset, which decried the activities of a variety of human-rights organizations.

Then, in January 2010, a major initiative was launched directly against the New Israel Fund (NIF), a US–Israel collaboration that has jumpstarted over 800 progressive civil society associations, and offers grants and services (through its capacity-building arm, Shatil) to a similar number of groups annually. This, particularly virulent, salvo was delivered by Im Tirtzu, then a relatively unknown student group with deep roots in the anti-Gaza disengagement movement, established to promote (in its own words) "the values of Zionism in Israel and to renew and reinstate Zionist discourse, thinking and ideology in order to secure the future of the Jewish people and the State of Israel and strengthen Israeli society in the challenges it faces."[5] It alleged that NIF-funded human- and civil-rights organizations had directly contributed negative information to the Goldstone Commission, which held Israel responsible for multiple violations of international law during the 2008–2009 military action in Gaza.[6]

From the perspective of its instigators, the campaign was highly successful. Although the charges against the NIF and the human-rights community were refuted systematically in several reports,[7] these details did not penetrate into the public consciousness. Continuous doubts were cast both on the credibility and loyalty of human-rights defenders; the heretofore fairly anonymous NIF was thrust into the role of an ignominious giant; the already pallid political left was further besmirched. And, while some organizations and influential individuals immediately stood up against the campaign and warned of its profound repercussions, most Israeli moderates either took it in their stride or tried to distance themselves from its targets.[8]

By mid-April 2010, it became clear that the assault on progressive civil society could not be dismissed as a one-time event. For the second time, Im Tirtzu launched an all-out attack on the human-rights community and the NIF, now focusing on the purported role some of these groups play in prosecuting Israeli officials for human-rights violations abroad.[9] This campaign, like its predecessors, was accompanied by a media blitz, which included print articles, posters, banners and songs (depicting the NIF and its grantees as enemies of the Israel Defense Forces); the personalization of the victims of these actions (former prime ministers, defense ministers and senior military officers); the mobilization of sympathetic Members of Knesset; and, simultaneously, demonstrations timed to coincide with Israel's memorial day.[10]

The response of the NIF and its family of organizations was far more assertive and professional in this round, highlighting not only the dangers inherent in a mounting campaign structured to undermine progressive associations in particular and civil society in general, but also its retrogressive implications for Israel's democracy. Nevertheless, within a short few months, Im Tirtzu had established itself as a key purveyor and guardian of a revised, exceedingly narrow, version of Zionism and the type of patriotism it entails. A clear divide had been created in the public mindset between the majority of Israelis, on the one hand, and human-rights organizations and their proponents, on the other.

In this environment, it was relatively easy to expand the scope of those under scrutiny beyond civil society organizations to the bastion of Israel's intelligentsia, its academic institutions. Once again, Im Tirtzu led the barrage, backed by the IZS and sympathetic politicians. Its founders, Ronen Shoval and Erez Tadmor, unearthed and updated a 2008 analysis of political science departments in an attempt to link scholars in this field with anti-Zionist and post-Zionist ideologies. The (methodologically deficient) report tried to prove that most courses on nationalism at Israeli universities were tainted by fundamentally flawed and disloyal attitudes toward the origins and actions of the state.[11]

These findings were prominently displayed in what had by then become the lead outlet of Im Tirtzu, *Ma'ariv*, and given additional exposure at an emergency meeting of the Education Committee of the Knesset, chaired by Member of Knesset Zevulun Orlev, which concluded with a recommendation to the Council on Higher Education that it review political science curricula.[12] The new campaign aroused the heretofore quiescent academic community, unleashing heated discussions on Social Science list-serves, a series of conferences on academic freedom, a plethora of op-eds in leading newspapers, and a growing public concern over renewed efforts to limit freedom of speech and opinion.[13]

The offensive against the academy continued throughout the summer of 2010, led this time by the IZS, which published a report devoted to the detailed scrutiny of the syllabi of departments of sociology.[14] The escalating friction peaked in the latter part of August, better known in Israel as the "cucumber season," when Im Tirtzu reentered the fray—dispatching a letter to the President of Ben-Gurion University demanding disciplinary action against tenured members of the political science department (who it accused of radical anti-Zionist activities including support of an academic boycott of Israel) and threatening to approach donors to desist from supporting the university should no such steps be taken forthwith. This particular initiative, unlike its predecessors, backfired: not only did the academic establishment (the Committee of University Presidents, the Israel Academy of Sciences, faculty from all Israeli institutions of higher learning) come out emphatically against Im Tirtzu's self-appointed thought brigade,[15] but key officials heretofore sympathetic to Im Tirtzu (such as Minister of Education Gideon Sa'ar who was the keynote speaker at its national convention earlier in the year) expressed reservations about their call for a boycott of the university in the Negev.[16]

At this point, yet another front against progressive voices was opened, this time aimed at social justice advocates. The lead role in this round was assumed by a loosely knit student group formed at Bar-Ilan University, operating under the name of the Forum for the Land of Israel, which spearheaded an additional attack on the NIF, this time focusing on its support for social change organizations advocating a more equitable distribution of dividends from newly discovered offshore natural gas reserves. This campaign sought to address an audience of entrepreneurs wary of increased government regulation of the market. In a brash series of ads, banners and posters, the NIF was accused of favoring "Arab" (a reference to the Israeli–Egyptian gas agreements ensconced in the 1979 peace treaty) over Israeli gas, and intimating that Professor Eitan Sheshinsky, the head of a government-appointed review body, was unfit because his wife was associated with the NIF.[17]

The natural gas episode was far from effective, suffering from two major flaws. First, substantively, it drew a direct link between right-wing positions and the financial interests of a small clique of industrialists widely believed to have close connections with decision-makers. It became difficult, if not impossible, to explain why patriotism coincided with enhancing the profits of these stakeholders at the expense of the general public. Second, tactically, the personal attack on Professor Sheshinsky (which also included a demonstration outside his home) only invited support from unexpected quarters, including the Minister of Finance Yuval Steinitz and the Attorney-General.[18]

At the end of the summer, another link was added to the ever-expanding neo-nationalist net, in the shape of performers and artists, following a petition in which some members of the Cameri Theatre announced that they would not appear in the new Center for the Performing Arts in the settlement of Ariel. Just before the Jewish New Year in September 2010, verbal battles between proponents and opponents of these actors, playwrights and directors abounded.[19]

The autumn of 2010 witnessed the further dissemination of barbs aimed at progressive segments of Israeli society, with special attention devoted to Arab citizens of Israel. In early December, over 350 rabbis on the government payroll signed an appeal to the public to refrain from selling or renting flats to Arabs; they subsequently backed demonstrations in various cities in support of this prohibition. Counter-protests and petitions organized by pluralist groups both in Israel and abroad accentuated the increasingly charged climate in the public arena.[20]

The first part of 2011 followed a similar script, with ongoing reminders by various neo-nationalist groups of the supposed transgressions of progressive civil society and its defenders. The publication of a new Im Tirtzu report, this time on Arab funding of "anti-Israel" organizations, served as an incentive for heated debates in the Knesset (although it was greeted with a certain amount of derision in the mainstream press).[21] The same cannot be said for the renewed campaign against the NIF and human-rights organizations in the wake of the publication of an article by Justice Richard Goldstone raising questions about the intentionality of Israeli attacks against civilians in the

Gaza operation, the centerpiece of the heavily disputed report of the commission he headed.[22] Indeed, the revived debate over the Goldstone Report provided an opportunity for another media and public barrage against progressive forces in the country. By then, the lines of socio-political division that had been demarcated since the 2009 elections by a series of nationalistically inspired anti-democratic activities had reached a new peak,[23] accompanied for the first time by overtly anti-democratic legislation which persisted into 2012.[24]

Intriguingly, this barrage began to evoke a democratically inspired pushback, first evident in the social justice protests which swept the country in the summer of 2011. Drawing on a civil backlash against neo-liberal policies and the high cost of living they have generated, these events have led to a redirection of public discourse and a resurgence of citizen empowerment; they have not succeeded, to date, in stemming anti-democratic trends.

These can no longer be treated as either haphazard or ineluctable. Their purpose is to delineate and then denigrate what they define as the domestic enemy. Their dynamic progression has targeted growing segments of Israeli society and labeled them as an elitist and unproductive intelligentsia with questionable patriotic credentials. By extension, any group promoting social justice and social change—from refugee rights and the advancement of women to freedom of the press—got trapped in this net. For exactly this reason, these actions constitute an unprecedented and purposeful assault on Israel's democracy.

De-democratization: The method

The escalating dynamic of democratic recession, protestations aside, is neither random nor unplanned. The pattern of attacks has followed a clear, repetitive formula purposely designed to enhance its neo-nationalist message. Each phase has consisted of several distinct, interconnected components. The first has involved the publication of a "research" brief, followed, second, by a media expose designed to magnify the critique and fuel additional commentary. Virtually simultaneously, a third element has been put in place: a public campaign against specific groups or coalitions identified as particularly untrustworthy by the domestic opponents of critical voices (including demonstrations, the mobilization of social networks, paid ads, internet banners, posters and derogatory billboards placed at major thoroughfares). Fourth, the public outreach has relied heavily on the personalization of the anti-liberal message, focusing for effect on the demonization of one or more individuals as the human embodiment of the positions that are being discredited.[25]

The fifth ingredient of anti-liberal offensives has centered on decision-makers: legislators, government ministers, and key officials have been recruited to give official weight to the attacks and to translate them into policy. The main focus of activities has been the Knesset. Several full-scale debates on civil society, the political orientation of academic institutions and protest groups have been held both in the plenum and in specific committees. One attempt to establish a parliamentary commission of inquiry into the NIF in early 2010 was thwarted; a second, to create a parliamentary commission of inquiry into the funding of human-rights organizations, is still pending (although it is doubtful that it will be brought to a vote during the tenure of the eighteenth Knesset).[26]

Far more problematic has been a spate of legislative initiatives intent on constraining personal liberties and democratic rights. The first attempt to limit civil society organizations came in the form of a bill introduced by Likud Member of Knesset Ze'ev Elkin, the majority whip, aimed at reducing foreign government funding of Israeli NGOs. A massive lobby effort conducted by a broad coalition of human-rights organizations succeeded in watering down some of its provisions, but it was nevertheless passed into law in February 2011.[27] Additional bills to further limit or tax foreign government funding of Israeli NGOs were introduced, but have yet to be brought to a vote.

The so-called Elkin law opened the door for a flood of proposed bills which possess a distinctly retrogressive aura. Although many of these initiatives—introduced not only by members of the coalition from the Likud, Israel Beiteinu, the National Union, and the National Religious Party, but also by leading members of Kadima, the main opposition party—were at first perceived by many observers more as political declarations, it is now apparent that a legislative transformation is in the making. Between January 2010 and January 2012, thirty-four anti-democratic laws were tabled; seven completed the full legislative process and became law and a further nine passed preliminary readings and are at various stages of approval. Among the bills enacted during this period is one that imposes fines on publicly funded institutions permitting discussions of the Palestinian narrative associated with the foundation of the State of Israel in 1948 (The Nakba Law), another that legalizes thinly veiled discriminatory restrictions against access to communal settlements (Acceptance to Communities Law), yet another that makes it an offense to call for a boycott against Israel or settlement products (The Boycott Prohibition Law), as well as several that limit civil liberties (Revoking Citizenship due to Conviction Law; the Law to Prevent Infiltration; and an amendment to the Citizenship Law prohibiting residency to Palestinian spouses of Israeli citizens). Additional initiatives are at advanced stages of legislation, including one which significantly raises compensation paid for libel without proof of damages and another which would restrict public petitions to the High Court of Justice.

The formal dimension of the current assault on progressive groups and opinions provides them with substantial traction and durability. It has been buttressed by constant repetition. The working assumption of the strategists behind these campaigns has been that their effectiveness would be augmented if they continuously hammered away at their key message—in this instance, the abject disloyalty of certain civil society organizations and their funders and their collusion with Israel's most nefarious external detractors. By reinforcing this mantra by every available means, innuendo could be transformed into fact and the negative public image of liberal voices in the country would be entrenched.[28]

A tightly knit, coordinated set of associations has spearheaded the dissemination of this new brand of Israeli patriotism. These include Im Tirtzu, the Forum for the Land of Israel, the virtual network-based front of secular revisionist forces, Yisrael Sheli (My Israel), and several academic watchdogs (Israel Academia Monitor, Isracampus, and Campus Watch).[29] These relatively new groups are closely linked to other organizations with ties to the traditional national-religious right: NGO Monitor and the IZS, which have provided active support for their agenda through a variety of publications, public appearances, and training programs. The direct connection between NGO Monitor and the IZS is even closer: they share some board members, donors, methodologies, and outlooks. Both organizations have ties to the veteran Jerusalem Center for Public Affairs and to the conservative Shalem Center.[30] Tellingly, Moshe Klughaft, who until recently served as the public-relations advisor of Member of Knesset Ronit Tirosh, a vocal supporter of Im Tirtzu and the IZS and the originator of several anti-NGO bills, has been the main strategist for all the recent campaigns—regardless of who actually stood at the forefront.[31] Thus, the leaders of the attacks on progressive groups and opinions are an integral part of what is by now a dense interlocking network that reaches into the uppermost echelons of government and the Knesset today.[32]

These groups also share sources of funding, although they rarely stand up to minimum standards of transparency. Thus, while Im Tirtzu until recently received substantial support from the John Hagee Ministries and its subsidiary, Christians United for Israel,[33] many of its donations are funneled through the Central Fund for Israel (CFI), which also provides monies to many right-wing organizations and settler enterprises. The IZS gets the lion's share of its budget support from the Hudson Institute, while receiving private donations through CFI as well.[34] The funding map of the NGO Monitor is not dissimilar: several acknowledged major funders (in this case, as reported on its website, the somewhat elusive Harry Wechsler Foundation and a handful of private donors have consistently supported its activities), while it also enjoys backing from sources closely associated with both the Jerusalem Center for Public Affairs and the IZS.[35] The more ephemeral Forum for the Land of Israel has been even more circumspect in its disclosures, merely acknowledging anonymous donors and hiding behind their right to privacy.[36]

Above and beyond this mixture of foreign and local, acknowledged and hidden, Jewish and non-Jewish funding sources, which provided an estimated NIS 20 million for the anti-progressive public campaigns in 2010 alone, these have been buttressed by formal means as well. Buried in the 2011–2013 budget is an annual allocation of NIS 10 million for programs designed to promote Zionist activities by non-governmental organizations.[37] Within this framework, Im Tirtzu has been recruited to provide training courses for senior educational personnel organized and subsidized by the Ministry of Education.

Sociologically, the interlocking forces that have constructed a fortifying structural, financial, and public edifice for the neo-nationalist surge go beyond the national-religious (Ashkenazi, orthodox, middle class) base that supported similar initiatives in the past and continue to constitute the backbone of the settlement enterprise today. Many of the new activists are outspokenly secular, middle-class professionals hailing from the Tel Aviv area—heretofore considered the stronghold of progressive Israelis. They have been joined by segments of the Russian-speaking community, who share many of Avigdor Lieberman's political orientations. The more heterogeneous sociological aura these groups exude is a major instrument in conveying their call for fidelity as defined by uniformity.

De-democratization: The message

The widening effort to discredit critical progressive voices is but the tip of the iceberg. It is the outward, ever-intensifying, and constantly expanding expression of a much broader majoritarian project, which has a direct impact on Israel's democratic institutions, discourse and ethos. The recent public campaigns interlock and serve a common objective: the reconfiguration of societal norms and, by extension, the redefinition of the terms of membership in Israel's fragile and highly fractured society.

The essential pillar of this endeavor is the insistence on one, hegemonic, interpretation of what is good for Israel and hence of Israeli patriotism. This new nationalism views the state as the latter-day expression of the historic link between the Jewish people and the land of Israel. It equates loyalty to the state with an uncritical adherence to this worldview. Any deviation from this characterization is, by definition, not only unacceptable but also harmful to Israel and its interests. In this exclusivist mindset, allegiance to these precepts becomes the measure of good citizenship; there is neither room nor legitimacy for disagreements over substance.

The diversity of means to express identification with Israel and love for the country thus gives way to a uniformity test devoid of specific content. There is little place for exalting social heterogeneity in this outlook, nor for groups that convey Israel's essential multiculturalism.

The various components of this new patriotism emerge vividly from close scrutiny of both the text and the subtext of recent de-democratization efforts. The linchpin of this worldview is a renewed and officially sanctioned insularity: an ongoing stress on Israeli self-sufficiency as the main protection against an increasingly hostile world. This has been heightened in the aftermath of the democratically inspired upheavals in the Arab world, which commenced in December 2010 and have fomented great uncertainty in the Israeli body politic. Any consideration of regional or global concerns (let alone universal values) is deemed suspect; cooperation with foreign governments and international institutions is viewed as collaboration with anti-Israeli forces and fundamentally antithetical to the country's interests.

The narrow lens of self-encapsulation then becomes the basis for the promulgation of a series of tests imposed by the self-appointed guardians of this latter-day neo-nationalism. These include uncritical support for military actions, for the IDF itself, for more control over land and resources, and, ultimately, for a narrow, ethno-centric definition of Israeli identity. Here conformity with a Jewish characterization of the state has become the litmus test for Israel's domestic (as well as foreign) supporters. In a very real sense, the distinction between "those who are for us and those who are against us" in the global arena has been domesticated.[38]

The cumulative campaign against civil society in Israel has focused squarely on purported violations of this unfolding solidarity. Each segment of the anti-democratic onslaught has therefore narrowed in on one specific aspect of government policy, usually related to the Israeli occupation of Palestinian territories or Israeli military actions. By concentrating on the most political and heavily disputed issues surrounding Israeli policy and linking them to the work of human-rights and peace organizations, these campaigns have cast doubts not only on the overall credibility of these groups, but also on their legitimacy. They have also sought to create a divide between these organizations and their progressive counterparts dealing with issues of social change and social justice.

The current reformulation of the hegemonic narrative is binary in structure and divisive in practice. The tools developed during the progression of the current de-democratization process are designed to differentiate between fellow travelers, who are embraced, and others, who are increasingly defamed. In this very simplistic—yet undoubtedly effective—manner, where one stands has come to supersede what one thinks and any examination of the values one upholds.

Indeed, the most striking feature of this neo-nationalist surge lies precisely in what it lacks: any clear substance. Adherence to some ambiguous idea of an Israel demarcated by an undifferentiated Jewish solidarity is seen as the only steadfast test of membership in the collective. In this universe, there is no place for discussion over the future of the territories, social discrepancies, the status of Jerusalem, religious-secular tensions or, for that matter, any other issue on the public agenda. The identity of the protagonists becomes far more important than the validity of any arguments they might muster.[39] The redrawn public domain is marked by the almost total absence of content and by a consequent belittlement of supportive values. This new, exclusivist and homogenized, nationalism therefore cannot sustain real differences of opinion. From this perspective, the highly professional efforts of recent years seek to mold a more compliant, unquestioning Israeli public less inclined to challenge or defy hegemonic currents. This unfolding, affinity-based, mind-frame propels neo-nationalist activism, defines the contours of the monolithic discourse it seeks to impose, and delineates its intended outcomes.[40] It also, of necessity, shifts the discussion to a totally different level: one that relates to the foundations of Israel's very identity.

De-democratization: The causes

The de-democratization syndrome currently afflicting Israeli society is the outcome of a cumulative set of historical, organizational, behavioral, emotional, psychological, and political factors. The backdrop for this unfettered offensive on progressive groups rests, like so many schisms in Israeli society, in embedded differences surrounding the ongoing occupation and approaches to the resolution of the Israeli–Palestinian conflict. Its intensification cannot be detached from the growing isolation of Israel in the international arena in the wake of the Second Lebanon War and the Gaza operation in December 2008 and January 2009. Nor can its escalation be divorced from Palestinian moves to internationalize the resolution of the conflict through procuring the recognition of Palestinian independence in the United Nations. The almost complete international consensus against Israel's ongoing retention of territories captured in 1967, coupled with the inability to reach a durable accommodation, is therefore a direct cause for the demise in democratic adherence.

In contrast to prior representations of the division over the boundaries (and hence the nature) of Israel, the burgeoning neo-nationalism focuses less on the physical character of the state and more on the definition of its community. It offers a human rather than territorial formulation of the notion of a Greater Land of Israel, thereby sacrificing the democratic and civic character of the state in favor of its Jewish configuration.

The appeal to a patently exclusive version of the Israeli collective effectively stifles discussion on the consequences of continued rule over another people not only for the Palestinians, but also for Israel's own inner fabric. Since democratic norms can hardly be maintained at home over an extended period of time if civil and human rights stop at the Green Line, it is easier to bypass debates on this issue by highlighting the need to assure Jewish integrity and survival. Through this technique, it might be possible also to delay—if not to entirely obstruct—significant moves to create a Palestinian state alongside Israel. The security narrative that supported Israel's reluctance to resolve the conflict in the past has thus acquired an additional, communal, layer.

The modification of the public discourse has been facilitated by several contributing factors. On the emotive level, ingrained fear of international isolation has been exacerbated in recent years, especially in light of regional changes and the fact that in the twenty-first century there is far less tolerance in the global arena for the delay in realizing the Palestinian right to self-determination. The undermining of Israel's international standing in these circumstances has magnified the deep-seated fear of annihilation which has accompanied the country since its inception. The mobilization of this widespread sense of vulnerability and of the siege mentality that goes with it inevitably fosters a division of the world into enemies and friends, and encourages the internalization of these distinctions.

On the psychological level, the uncertainty inherent in this situation encourages a paranoia which not only instills a sense of constant insecurity, but also inculcates a profound suspicion of the other. By failing to make the distinction between critics and delegitimizers either at home or abroad, this sentiment provides tacit if not overt official backing for domestic efforts aimed at the identification—and persistent hounding—of perceived enemies within. The embedded intolerance for difference encompasses not only individuals and groups, but also ideas and opinions. It tends to peak when regional and global uncertainty rises, as in the case of the massive shifts in the geo-political context in the Middle East since the beginning of the so-called "Arab Spring." Indeed, the cessation of any serious Israeli–Palestinian discussions has highlighted the link between unpredictability in the region and rigidity at home. In the process, the willingness to celebrate diversity and entertain pluralism has diminished, rendering many Israelis more amenable to homogenous messages.

Some commentators have suggested that these trends may have been accelerated not only by events related to the ongoing conflict, but also by demographic shifts in Israeli society in recent years.[41] The growing percentage of religious and ultra-orthodox in the population has, indeed, buttressed parochial outlooks; the large immigration from the former Soviet Union has, in broad strokes, enhanced nationalist views. But such an essentialist explanation, deterministic by nature, is at best a reinforcing element in a broader process. At worst it is an excuse to avoid delving into the root causes of recent developments.

Much more significant are the institutional sources of de-democratization. The fundamental uncertainties that have plagued Israel, particularly since the commencement of negotiations with the Palestinians two decades ago, have been accompanied by no small measure of indecisiveness. These have contributed directly to endemic political instability and exacerbated problems of governance. The subsequent institutional fragility that has come to mark the public arena in Israel offers fertile ground for patriotic appeals as a replacement for organizational predictability. It also evokes considerable alienation from politicians in particular and the public sphere in general. These are well-known corollaries of weakening states—a phenomenon not heretofore associated with formal Israeli institutions.

The recent flourishing of neo-nationalist ideas has also inevitably benefited from the tangible contraction of moderate political forces in the formal arena. Indeed, the creation of Kadima as a purportedly centrist party willing to entertain some form of a two-state solution siphoned off votes from both Labor and Meretz on the eve of the 2006 elections. The collaboration of the Labor Party with the Sharon and Olmert governments during the last decade merely underscored its ideological indeterminacy, further reducing its public appeal and rendering peace-oriented outlooks with barely any representation following the Likud comeback in the 2009 ballot. The void left by the virtual collapse of the party-political left has enabled the unchecked proliferation of a conformist mindset. The absence of strong liberal forces in decision-making positions has, at the same time, shifted the progressive center of gravity to civil society organizations, making them an obvious target for stepped-up attacks in the name of the new patriotism.

There is, therefore, a clear political motivation behind the recent intensification of the anti-democratic surge. This trajectory is a direct outgrowth of the composition of the structure of power in the country and of the hubris that it engenders.[42] The denigration of progressive civil society serves the purpose of further enfeebling the already weakened left, ensures the electoral dominance of right-wing parties for some time to come, and, not coincidentally, prepares the ideological groundwork for the continuation of the conflict. From this perspective, what is taking place in the country today is not just the sum total of the historical, emotional, psychological, institutional, and political factors presently at work; it is the end result of a conscious policy designed and directed by those who now run the country.

The neo-nationalist delegitimization of civil society helps decision-makers shirk responsibility for Israel's deteriorating global position by shifting the onus to these groups, thus entrenching the current coalition in power and reducing the chances of a moderate electoral comeback. Since the quest for ongoing political control cannot be achieved by garnering public backing for major policy moves (especially since their number is limited and their contours are blurred), it is being aggressively pursued through other means in the realm of discourse and identity. These processes serve the immediate political interests of those in power and make the prospect of the resolution of the conflict even more remote.

Regardless of the relative importance attributed to design as opposed to process or circumstances, it is evident that attempts to stymie democratic pluralism are the result of a multiplicity of factors that have come together to nurture a climate of mounting xenophobia and intolerance. It is this mindset that transforms the traditional divisions between left and right into something different—a blatant challenge to Israel's normative underpinnings. It allows for constant assaults on Israel's democracy and might, if successful, threaten its viability.

De-democratization: The effects

The retrogressive dynamic engulfing Israeli society has affected several key dimensions of its democratic order. The first concerns civil liberties—and specifically the gradual erosion of the significance attributed to freedom of speech and association. The effort to silence divergent voices is central to the new nationalism. Therefore, the ongoing campaign against civil society organizations and academe focuses extensively on the purported illegitimacy of certain positions or statements—implying that freedom of speech is contingent on its content. Rebuttals to these allegations, however compelling, have failed to stem the tide.[43]

In the same vein, the purveyors of the new patriotism have been active in constricting (if not entirely prohibiting) demonstrations protesting governmental policies or official abuses. These restrictions are most apparent in the strong-arm tactics employed in the ongoing demonstrations against the security barrier and against Jewish settlement in Palestinian neighborhoods of East Jerusalem. They are also evident in repeated attempts to limit public protests by Arab citizens of Israel and in the reluctance to grant permits for *ad hoc* gatherings or vigils against specific Israeli actions (most notably the Israeli operation in Gaza in 2008–2009 and the flotilla incidents in the summer of 2010).

Israelis are hardly denied civil liberties—the public arena is both boisterous and diverse. Recent occurrences have, however, raised two interrelated warning signals, the first of which relates to the inequitable application of these freedoms depending on political outlooks (settler protests are given a wide berth; the same cannot be said of those who oppose their expansion or their very existence). The second concerns the glaring inability to distinguish between freedom of speech and incitement and between freedom of association and rebellion. This blurring of boundaries permits unfettered liberties on one side of the political divide and questions their exercise on the other. Together, these trends not only skew the perception of civil liberties, they also fuel a widespread reduction in the public's assessment of their centrality.[44]

The second negative effect of neo-nationalist efforts relates to the decreased commitment to the protection of minority rights—the litmus test of vibrant democracies. The new patriots have concentrated many of their arrows on the major Palestinian–Israeli civil rights groups, querying their intentions and undermining their credibility. In this atmosphere, it is hardly surprising that Israeli public opinion exhibits little tolerance for the different, the other, the diverse. Recent polls show alarming levels of suspicion and outright racism not only toward Arab citizens, but also toward other marginalized groups.[45] Israel's already debatable record in this regard is undermining its democratic credentials.

Third, the combination of prejudice against particular groups and disdain for individual liberties has a direct impact on the scope and content of public discourse. De-democratization efforts have consciously attempted to restrict the range of permissible debate. By persistently asserting that certain positions are akin to sedition, and hence beyond the bounds of acceptable discussion, they question the legitimacy of their adherents. In the process, the lines of internal debate have been redrawn, focusing increasingly on standards of patriotism and fidelity rather than on substantive disagreements, although social protests of the summer of 2011 deflected attention to socioeconomic issues which can no longer be ignored.

Ironically, the campaign to remold the contours of public discourse has generated vigorous discussion on the nature of democratic deliberation. And, while in this regard the constriction of formal political spaces has yielded a flourishing discussion on its limits (which is being carried out along lines that diverge from the traditional left–right divide), the diversity of discussion on a variety of central issues on the national agenda has diminished.

The containment of public discourse has made it easier, fourth, to mount a systematic campaign to weaken—if not entirely dismantle—key organizations in civil society. It is precisely the diversity of these groups that provides the structural basis for democratic societies. Their number and heterogeneity assure the essential pluralism of the democratic order. The purposeful efforts to limit sources of funding, impose additional bureaucratic restrictions, and curtail fields of activity—especially of human rights organizations—touch on the tangible foundations of democratic societies. Tampering with the ability of certain civil society groups to function of necessity compromises the structural robustness of Israel's democracy. Indeed, the institutional ramifications of the de-democratization campaign are particularly severe. A shift in policy or in public outlooks may reopen debates and lift constraints on societal action; the reconstruction of civil institutions is a far more prolonged and complex task.

Finally, recent de-democratization initiatives have undermined the already tenuous consensus on the rules of the game. The ability to live together while disagreeing, vigorously and passionately, is essential to democratic societies. It is based on an adherence to the rule of law and on the understanding that its provisions are applied equitably to all citizens. These binding rules are value-driven: they assume agreement on the basic elements of the democratic ethos.

The orchestrated assault on progressive organizations and viewpoints has utilized rules and regulations selectively and manipulatively. Its purveyors have attempted to create a dual codex: one for the defenders of their version of Israel and another for its critics. Thus, while they have skirted existing laws and trodden on the edge of (if not beyond) prevailing behavioral guidelines, they are unwilling to accede the right of others to employ the full range of opportunities and strategies they themselves use.[46] Compliance with the regulations guiding normative behavior is uneven at best.

The result of these shifts in the democratic foundations of the Israeli polity has been to encourage a public airing of the benefits and the drawbacks of democracy for Israel. Besides the well-worn revival of discussions on the compatibility of the Jewish and democratic elements of Israeli identity, doubts have increasingly been cast on the significance of the country's democratic framework. It has become fashionable in certain circles to debunk democracy and to maintain that fears about Israel's democratic deterioration are but a new form of unfounded mud-slinging.[47]

These changes have assisted in recasting the meaning of democracy to conform to the neo-nationalist narrative. Stripped of its concern for minorities and their rights, it is increasingly interpreted in simplistic terms as majority rule. In these circumstances, it is also potentially expendable. When pitted against survival, it can easily be sacrificed if the latter is at risk. It is hardly surprising, therefore, that over a third of the Israeli public is unsure whether Israel needs its democracy at all.[48] Given the significance of democracy to Israel's capacity to endure under constant external pressure for over six decades, this is indeed a sorry commentary on the country's present mindset.

Israel is now undergoing profound upheavals which have serious ramifications for its internal cohesion and its external standing. What began as a series of targeted campaigns against strongholds of diversity is fast developing into a generalized phenomenon which centers on a struggle over the redefinition of Israel's identity. The chipping away at its pluralistic core—let alone its inclusionary veneer—is contributing to a fundamental confrontation over priorities and guiding values.

De-democratization: The reaction

Recent anti-democratic propensities initially served to intensify processes of disengagement from public affairs that were already in motion. In a mutually reinforcing manner, disenchantment with politics and the political and a sense of reduced efficacy magnified the impact of precisely those forces that promote exclusionary approaches, further expediting withdrawal from the public arena and its concerns.[49] This cycle reduced the involvement of critical voices (both within Israel and in the Jewish world),[50] with a view to engendering a far more quiescent and less engaging public sphere. A democratic reawakening, however, facilitated not only by the social justice movement but also by a growing concern over the implications of democratic recession, has begun to emerge.

It has taken some time for democratic forces in Israel (and their Jewish counterparts abroad) to grasp the enormity of the threats to Israel's democratic character. Responses to the various stages of the de-democratization campaign have taken place on several distinct levels. The first focuses on addressing the details of particular accusations and is largely confined to targeted groups and their supporters. Thus, those under extremist scrutiny have spent inordinate energy explaining—and often refuting—allegations such as their connection with the Goldstone Commission, the global BDS movement, or particular foreign funders. These reactions inevitably possess an apologetic flavor. Yet they are necessary not only to set the record straight, but also to grapple with the familiar neo-nationalist tactic of utilizing repetition to selectively present, distort or actually manufacture facts, and thus to denigrate and discredit opponents.

Very quickly, however, the responses of civil society organizations and their supporters also moved to a second level, one which relates to the heart of the new discourse: loyalty to the state. This framing begs the essential question of the definition of the state and its character, unleashing, once again, an intense public discussion which is as old as Israel itself. Tellingly, however, since this renewed debate has come together with hegemonic attempts to equate critical approaches with efforts to undermine Israel's existence, it has compelled serious thought about the distinction between support of Israel's legitimacy and disagreement over its nature. Progressive efforts to come to terms with these complexities have generated both profound reconsideration and at times painstaking refinement of positions, as well as not insignificant internal contestation—processes not always shared by their critics.[51]

The way this debate has been conducted has led to the development of a third level of response, one which centers on the limits of democratic freedom and consequently on the status of Israel's democratic order.[52] This has evoked a broader discussion on Israel's democratic viability—regardless of political orientation. It has also unleashed a tangible democratic upsurge within Israel and in the Jewish world.

The locus of the consolidation of this emerging democratic front is civil society. Its core members are the main peace, civil rights and human-rights organizations, which have been joined by a wide variety of social justice groups, academic networks, artists and performers, environmental groups, and grassroots initiatives. These have been reinforced by a spate of new, loosely formed coalitions that have sprouted up on the local as well as the national level, backed by social justice groups that survived after the 2011 protests. The by-now symbolically pivotal gathering of young activists that assemble every Friday to protest Jewish settlement in the Sheikh Jarrah quarter of Jerusalem has become the source of inspiration for several incipient movements (such as their campus-based offshoot Defenders of Democracy, the more politically oriented *Smol*—"Left," and the newly formed Democratic Camp, which seeks to coalesce many of these groups). These have been joined by a variety of organizations (the National Left is but one), which are attempting to give more formal political expression to the various manifestations of democratic activism.[53]

The still amorphous yet increasingly conscious civil society-based effort to rally civic voices is gaining traction in other quarters as well. It has been augmented by the establishment of constantly growing social networks that have formed an articulate and vibrant virtual democratic community in the country.[54] Leading opinion-shapers have joined the fray, not only by extending their support to local initiatives, but also by highlighting the centrality of democratic issues in the public arena. There have been more petitions, symposia, conferences, op-eds, and debates in the media on the topic in recent months than ever in recent memory. The Israeli progressive blogosphere has never been so engaged or vocal as it is today. In fact, the neo-nationalist campaign has succeeded in reinvigorating what has been for far too long Israel's decidedly dormant and despondent liberal public.

The revitalization of democratic forces provided one of the key foundations for the eruption of the social uprising in the summer of 2011, resulting in a reinforcement of civic efficacy and a sense of empowerment within civil society. Although substantial concrete gains have been very slow in coming, the turmoil surrounding the demand for social justice has provided a turning point in popular engagement in the public sphere. Since then, civil society groups have responded to every single domestic issue—from the segregation of women to growing clashes around issues of religion and state.

In many respects, the activation of civil spaces stands in stark contrast to the contraction evident in the official political arena. It is also, however gradually, beginning to penetrate the formal sphere. The democratic awakening, although purveyed primarily by a handful of progressive Members of Knesset, is limited to neither opposition circles nor the traditional left of the political spectrum. It does have important advocates in the coalition and the government. These extend deep into the core of the Likud, whose revisionist elements have been alarmed by the curtailment of civil liberties and have been outspoken in their defense of democratic rights. Thus, even those who disagree strongly with homegrown critics of Israeli policies (Dan Meridor, Reuven Rivlin, Benny Begin, Michael Eitan, and Moshe Arens) have rallied to their support. True to the legacy of their intellectual mentor, Ze'ev Jabotinsky, they are committed to maintaining Israel as an open society.[55]

The non-partisan movement to save Israeli democracy is very much in its infancy. But it is gathering momentum in the face of the constant attacks of extremist groups (especially the violent settler group *Tag M'hir*—Price Tag—that has employed violent tactics against Palestinians and key members of Israel's left), and the growing discontent with socioeconomic inequities and religious coercion. This is still a decidedly asymmetrical struggle, but one which is beginning to encompass broader segments of Israel's population and to redefine the lines of debate both within the country and in the Jewish world.

In fact, in many respects, the upsurge of democratic discussions inside Israel actually parallels the coalescence of progressive Jewish alliances abroad. The formation of J Street and the rise of "pro-Israel, pro-peace" voices in the United States as a counterpoint to a Jewish establishment bent on indiscriminately defending whatever Israel does provided the inspiration for the creation of J-Call in Europe, the organization of a J-List in Australia, and the beginning of similar efforts in South Africa, Great Britain, and Argentina.[56] These initiatives have in common a commitment to Israel's long-term interests; they also, significantly, share a firm belief in the connection between Israel's humanistic and democratic complexion and its ability to survive and thrive. In a very compelling way, they link Jewish identity in the twenty-first century to an avowedly liberal worldview and seek to explicate the precise connection between the values of equality, justice, and tolerance and contemporary Jewish existence.[57]

Ironically, therefore, the targeting of civil associations has actually enhanced their importance as defenders of democracy and bearers of change. The fact that the new nationalists have succeeded in arousing a multiplicity of civic voices within the country is beginning to redefine the lines of debate both inside Israel and in the Jewish world. It is also indicative of the vibrancy of the approaches these liberal advocates embrace and of their potential power.

Democracy and de-democratization: Some implications

The crackdown on alternate voices in Israel is taking place within what is still a democratic framework where the influence garnered in civil society can yet make a difference. But this escalating dynamic does constitute a real threat to the country's still fragile democratic framework.

The recent campaigns conducted in the name of the new nationalism have had extremely disconcerting immediate outcomes. Conceptually, there is a palpable inability to distinguish between dissent (so vital to the flourishing of an open society) and delegitimization (which undercuts its very foundations). Democracies generally know well how to defend themselves: those who diverge from the mainstream are protected and embraced; those who debunk the system in its entirety are marginalized and isolated. But when these differences become blurred, as is happening in Israel today, then the vitality of the public sphere is substantially eroded and its democratic elements are severely compromised.[58]

The practical extension of this confusion is to augment the prevailing propensity to conflate criticism of Israeli policies and actions with assaults on its right to exist. Domestically, this tendency lumps together debates over the character of the state with efforts to question its basic legitimacy. Externally, this trend leads to the dismissal of any commentary on Israeli positions as akin to a rejection of Israel itself. Policy-makers, observers, and the public at large constantly make the mistake of placing Israel's empathetic critics in the same basket as its worst enemies. Nothing can be more damaging for promoting Israeli interests abroad or for fostering positive change at home.

These results, largely an outgrowth of Israel's response to concerns over its policies and its continued presence in the occupied territories, exacerbate the undermining of Israel's democratic credibility and are undoubtedly harmful to its international standing. Without its democratic credentials, its already limited ability to maneuver in the global arena will be further constrained. Israel's capacity to muster support, to maintain economic and cultural relations with other countries, and, ultimately, to survive in a globalized world depends increasingly on its continued membership in the democratic world. Indeed, democracy has been in the past—and continues to be today—its most important ticket to acceptability in the international community. The prospect of global closure has widespread consequences not only for Israel but also for the stability of the region in its entirety. Thus, while isolation is a key cause of Israel's democratic recession, the consequence of this process is even more deleterious: it undermines the normative basis for its vital international backing.

The specter of democratic failure is equally disastrous domestically. It threatens to condemn the next generation of Israelis to a form of parochial self-encapsulation devoid of possibilities for internal regeneration and constructive external engagement. In this profoundly existential sense, should Israel abandon its democratic character, it runs the risk of losing its being.

The outcome of these developments is increased bifurcation within Israel and in the ranks of its supporters elsewhere.[59] What started with disagreements over the occupation has gone far beyond disputes over policy. The effects of continued rule over another people have infiltrated Israel's own core. Two competing orientations are vying with each other for dominance over the heart and soul of the country. The prospects for re-democratization are inherent in this tension: the revitalization of civic engagements harbors the possibility, if transferred to the political sphere, of stemming the neo-nationalist tide. Pressure from Jewish communities elsewhere, coupled with the urging of democratic states, can play a significant role in this process.

The tug-of-war over Israel's democratic institutions is the battleground between diverging worldviews. This divide is reflective of the depth of the current debate—one which focuses on the values and norms guiding Israeli society and the concrete steps that these entail. This soul-searching is not simply an Israeli affair: it touches on the essence of the contemporary global

Jewish community, which in this century lives almost entirely in the free world.

The issue, then, is who Israel is and what identity it assumes for itself and for those who care about its future. How this discussion is conducted and the results it yields will determine Israel's democratic viability and hence its survival. The reaffirmation of the principles of equality, pluralism, justice, and peace which informed the creation of the state and sustained its democracy to date is the only way of ensuring its vibrancy, decency, humanity, and, hence, durability.

Notes

1 In a recent poll, 56 percent of a random sample of Israelis agreed that "the whole world is against us" and 77 percent believed that "it doesn't matter what Israel does." Ephraim Yaar and Tamar Hermann, *Peace Index—August 2010*, Tel Aviv: Tel Aviv University, and Jerusalem: The Israel Democracy Institute, 2010.
2 Tamar Hermann, *The Israeli Peace Movement: A Shattered Dream*, New York: Cambridge University Press, 2009.
3 The publication of a series of papers by Arab intellectuals and leaders depicting their conception of the state helped fuel this image. See Sarah Ozacky Lazar and Mustafa Kabha (eds), *Between Vision and Reality: The Vision Papers of the Arabs in Israel, 2006–2007*, Jerusalem: The Citizens' Accord Forum between Jews and Arabs in Israel, 2008 [in Hebrew].
4 The Institute for Zionist Studies and NGO Monitor, "Conditional Sovereignty: The Scope of Foreign Government Support for Political Organizations in Israel," published in Hebrew and then in English under the title: "Trojan Horse: The Impact of European Government Funding for Israeli NGOs." Available at <http://www.ngo-monitor.org/article/trojan_horse_the_impact_of_european_government_funding_for_israeli_ngos>.
5 Im Tirtzu (If You Will It): Rebuilding a Zionist Society <http://imti.org.il/en>, 29 August 2010.
6 Im Tirtzu, "The Influence of the New Israel Fund Organizations on the Goldstone Report." Available at <www.israelbehindthenews.com/library/pdfs/NIFGoldstone.pdf>.
7 A. Paz-Fuchs, "Im Tirtzu—We Will Invent the Facts," 18 February 2010 [in Hebrew]. For an English summary: "Fact Checking the Anti-NIF Report: Systematic Omission and Distortion of Data," *Coteret*, 10 February 2010. Also see Keshev, the Center for the Protection of Democracy in Israel, "Im Tirtzu: If You Will It … Or Just Full of It?" <www.keshev.org.il/en/media-analyses/if-you-will-it.ht> [in Hebrew].
8 On the first week of the attack, over 250 leading opinion-makers published an ad in several newspapers in support of the New Israel Fund and its work; multiple op-eds appeared in the press and the electronic media.
9 Im Tirtzu, "The New Israel Fund: Prosecution of Senior Israeli Officials," April 2010 [in Hebrew].
10 Among those who came out in support of Im Tirtzu were Members of Knesset Ronit Tirosh, Othniel Schneler, Zeev Elkin, Anastasia Michaeli, and Ze'ev Elkin. They took the lead in proposing bills outlawing organizations involved in appeals to universal jurisdiction and supporting the global BDS movement respectively.
11 Im Tirtzu, "Anti-Zionist Bias in Political Science Departments in Israeli Universities" April 2010, in Hebrew. This report later influenced the findings of an evaluation committee to assess departments of political science, which singled out

Ben-Gurion University for political bias. See Tamar Trabelsi-Hadad, "Recommendation: Shut Down 'Leftist' Department," *YNet*, 23 November 2011. Available at <www.ynetnews.com/articles/0,7340,L-4152161,00.html>.

12 For details, see Protocol No. 201, The Education, Sport and Culture Committee of the Knesset, 28 April 2010 [in Hebrew].

13 The most vibrant exchanges occurred on the Social Science-Israel list-serve, the key vehicle for interchange among social scientists in the country.

14 The IZS study, methodologically more sophisticated than its Im Tirtzu counterpart, underscored the purported post-Zionist bias of key sociology departments, and especially those at Tel Aviv and Ben-Gurion universities. For the English version, see "Post Zionism in the Academy," The Institute for Zionist Strategies. Available at <http://izsvideo.org/papers/PostZionismAcademia2010>.

15 Paid ads were placed in major newspapers on 20 August 2010 by the Israel Academy of Arts and Sciences and by the Senior Faculty Association at Israeli universities.

16 See "Im Tirzu Threatens BGU Donations," *The Jerusalem Post,* 17 August 2010. Available at <www.jpost.com/Israel/Article.aspx?id=185016>.

17 The natural gas campaign, which continued until the spring of 2011, when the Sheshinsky Committee recommendations were enacted into law by an overwhelming majority of the Knesset, filled the economic pages of the media for many months. The opening response against the attack was spearheaded by Michael Melchior, the head of the Forum for Citizen Action, a diverse group of organizations opposed to the low dividend structure favoring the holders of natural gas concessions. See <http://www.themarker.com/tmc/article.jhtml?ElementId=skira20 100819_1185281> [in Hebrew].

18 See <http://www.ynet.co.il/articles/0,7340,L-3943675,00.html> [in Hebrew].

19 An informal group of writers, poets, artists, and senior academics (many holders of the prestigious Israel prize) took the lead not only in the public outcry against efforts to coerce actors to appear in Ariel, but subsequently in a series of initiatives against anti-racist legislation, rabbinical intervention in political affairs and, more recently, in the campaign to support a UN declaration of a Palestinian state. This group does not have a website or a Facebook account. Its coordinator is the author Sefi Rachlevsky and prominent in the group are political scientist Yaron Ezrahi, educator Gaby Salomon, artist Larry Abramson, and playwright Yehoshua Sobol.

20 For an example of one petition, initiated by university lecturers, to Prime Minister Netanyahu to intervene against the rabbis, see <http://www.haaretz.co.il/hasite/spages/1198576.html?more=1> [in Hebrew]. Over a thousand rabbis, mostly in the United States, signed a petition decrying the rabbis' appeal.

21 Im Tirtzu, "The Support of Arab States and Foundations for Organization Acting Against Israeli Policy and the IDF," 11 January 2011 [in Hebrew]. For a particularly harsh critique, see Larry Derfner, "Rattling the Cage: Im Tirtzu's Spectacle of Falsehood," *The Jerusalem Post*, 19 January 2011. Available at <http://www.jpost.com/Opinion/Columnists/Article.aspx?id=204393>.

22 Richard Goldstone, "Reconsidering the Goldstone Report on Israel and War Crimes," *The Washington Post*, 1 April 2011. Available at <http://www.washingtonpost.com/opinions/reconsidering-the-goldstone-report-on-israel-and-war-crimes/2011/04/01/AFgl11JC_story.html>.

23 For an initial listing, see the special edition of *Ha'ir*, no. 1553, 9 July 2010 [in Hebrew].

24 For an updated list of anti-democratic proposals and bills that have completed the legislative process, see the website of The Association for Civil Rights in Israel <http://www.acri.org.il/en>.

25 Thus, the initial attack of Im Tirtzu used a crude caricature of the author of this chapter, Naomi Chazan, as a means of linking the New Israel Fund which she heads to the Goldstone Commission. This was followed up by a highly personalized

ad campaign depicting her with a horn on her forehead (*keren* in Hebrew also means fund). The same type of demonization was used in April 2011, without the horn, in the follow-up campaign.

26 The motions to establish a parliamentary commission of inquiry on the funding of human-rights organizations was introduced in mid-January by Member of Knesset Faina Kirshenbaum of Israel Beiteinu and a similar motion was introduced by Member of Knesset Danny Danon of the Likud. It was approved by the Knesset committee on 31 January 2011. The proposal was not returned to the plenum before the spring break because of internal opposition within the Likud. For one example, see Yossi Verter, "If the Likud Mimics Israel Beiteinu, Our Chances to Win the Next Elections are Minimal," *Haaretz*, 21 January 2011. Available at <http://www.haaretz.co.il/hasite/spages/1210922.html> [in Hebrew].

27 For a specific breakdown of the status of particular initiatives, see "Anti-Democratic Legislation" <www.acri.org.il/en/tag/in-the-knesset> [in Hebrew].

28 This strategy is clear in an article by Eitan Dor-Shav, one of the strategists of the initial Im Tirtzu campaign. See "There is No Substitute for a Personal Campaign," *Makor Rishon*, no. 653, 12 February 2010 [in Hebrew].

29 See <www.myisrael.com>, which has over 40,000 followers. For further analysis, see "The Digital Soldiers of the Right," *The Marker*, 13 April 2011, p. 37 [in Hebrew].

30 NGO Monitor was, at the outset, housed within the Jerusalem Center for Public Affairs and received direct funding through JCPA channels.

31 On the role of Moshe Klughaft, see "Lobbyist or Advisor?" Available at <http://www.calcalist.co.il/local/articles/0,7340,L-3476201,00.html?dcRef=ynet> [in Hebrew]. Klughaft is also one of the owners of the publicity firm EDK, which produced the materials for several anti-NIF campaigns, most notably that related to natural gas.

32 Thus, Natan Sharansky and Moshe Ya'alon, for a while senior fellows at the Shalem Center, also served on the advisory board of the Institute for Zionist Strategies; Gerald Steinberg, the president of NGO Monitor, was a fellow of the Jerusalem Center for Public Affairs and acts as a legislative advisor to Likud Member of Knesset Ze'ev Elkin, who has been at the forefront of the legislation against progressive organizations. Ron Dermer, Prime Minister Netanyahu's political advisor, and Michael Oren, the ambassador to the US, were both fellows at Shalem.

33 For an in-depth analysis of the sources of funding of Im Tirtzu, see "The Surprising Sponsor of Im Tirtzu," *Calcalist*, 18 August 2010, pp. 2–3 [in Hebrew]. Also see <www.hahem.co.il/friendsofgeorge/?p.=1346> [in Hebrew].

34 Uri Blau, "Zionist Strategy With Foreign Funding," *Haaretz Magazine*, 24 February 2012, pp. 18–19.

35 Uri Blau, "Who Monitors the Monitor?" *Haaretz*, 10 February 2012, pp. 18–20.

36 For further information, see "John Hagee to Halt Im Tirtzu Funding," *The Jerusalem Post*, 24 August 2010.

37 Government decision 2049 of 15 July 2010.

38 For an excellent analysis of this tendency, see C. Strenger, "In the Circle of Paranoia," *Haaretz*, 31 December 2010 [in Hebrew].

39 A telling example of this discourse may be found in an op-ed written by the head of Im Tirtzu, Ronen Shoval, "Pluralism, Not McCarthyism," *Haaretz*, 13 September 2010 [in Hebrew].

40 There is a vibrant debate in the press and in academic circles on whether the current climate contains similarities to the McCarthy era in the United States or to fascism in Europe. For a summary, see U. Misgav, "Fascism? Here?!" *Yediot Aharonot* (Shabbat Magazine), 15 October 2010, pp. 6–9 [in Hebrew]. For one example of these many articles, see D. Shomsky, "Im Tirtzu (If You Will It) or If You Don't," *Haaretz*, 12 September 2010 [in Hebrew].

41 The propensity of immigrants from the former Soviet Union to support right-wing parties has become a standard assumption in Israeli politics during the past two

decades, although there are growing grounds to reassess this viewpoint. For a closer analysis of the effects of the Russian-speaking vote, see the various analyses in Asher Arian and Michal Shamir (eds), *The Elections in Israel, 2006*, New Brunswick, NJ: Transaction Press, 2008.

42 This analysis was presented in a public lecture by Galia Golan at the Interdisciplinary Center in Herzliya, 5 September 2010. A similar interpretation was conveyed in private discussions with Mordechai Kremnitzer of the Israel Democracy Institute in Jerusalem.

43 David Newman, "Thoughts on Academic Freedom at Pessah," *The Jerusalem Post*, 17 April 2011. Available at <http://www.jpost.com/Opinion/Op-EdContributors/Article.aspx?id=217024>.

44 A series of polls have highlighted the conditionality attributed not only to freedom of speech and association, but also to human-rights organizations. For a good summary, see Asher Arian, Tamar Hermann, Yuval Lebel, Michael Philippov, Hila Zaban, and Anna Knafelman, *Auditing Israeli Democracy: Democratic Values in Practice*, Jerusalem: The Israel Democracy Institute, November 2010 [in Hebrew].

45 A recent poll conducted by veteran pollster Mina Zemah demonstrates the ongoing sectarian nature of Israeli groups and highlights a pattern of sustained intergroup prejudice between Ashkenazi, Sephardi and immigrants from Russia and Ethiopia. It also indicates an understanding that, despite the persistence of deepseated intolerance and discrimination, the principle of equality is highly valued. See *Yediot Yerushalayim*, 29 September 2010, pp. 14–20 [in Hebrew].

46 One example is the suit brought by Im Tirtzu for NIS 2.5 million against the Facebook group, Im Tirtzu—A Fascist Movement, formed to debunk its efforts.

47 For one example of this approach to critiques of his work, see Gerald Steinberg, "Israel's Academic Left on the Attack," *The Jerusalem Post*, 17 May 2010. Available at <http://www.jpost.com/Opinion/Op-EdContributors/Article.aspx?id=175810>.

48 A poll conducted by Mina Zemah highlights these issues: 55 percent of a random sample advocated limiting freedom of speech; only 63 percent thought that Arab citizens should have the right to vote; and 26 percent preferred a strong leader over one subject to Knesset oversight. See *Yediot Aharonot*, 15 October 2010, p. 9 [in Hebrew].

49 The Israel Democracy Index of 2008 was devoted to this issue. See Arian, Hermann, Atmor, Hadar, and Zaban, *Auditing Israel's Democracy, 2008*. Available at <http://www.idi.org.il/sites/english/ResearchAndPrograms/The Israeli Democracy Index/Documents/2008DemocracyIndex.pdf>.

50 See Peter Beinart, *The Crisis of Zionism*, New York: Times Books, 2012, and his earlier article, "The Failure of the American Jewish Establishment," *New York Review of Books*, 10 June 2010. Available at <http://www.nybooks.com/articles/archives/2010/jun/10/failure-american-jewish-establishment/?pagination=false>.

51 For example, see the New Israel Fund principles codified in July 2010 <www.nif.org/about/new-israel-fund-principles.html>, which have created substantial discussion not only in the general public, but also within the progressive community in Israel and abroad.

52 For one example, see A. Carmon, M. Kremnitzer, and Y. Stern, "A Real Danger: Here and Now," *Yediot Aharonot*, 31 January 2011 [in Hebrew].

53 A variety of efforts are being examined to establish a liberal or democratic electoral alliance including Labor and Meretz, to bring together all progressive forces in a Jewish–Arab party proposed by former Speaker of the Knesset Avraham Burg (tentatively called *Shai*—the Israeli Left), or to create a coalition of groups left of Labor, including Meretz, the Green Movement, and segments of Hadash.

54 Some examples include Lo Nistom, Im Tirtzu—A Fascist Movement, and a series of blogs, such as the more veteran *Ha'oketz*, *Coteret*, and the new *+972*.

55 One example is an interview with Knesset Speaker Reuven Rivlin, "Israel's Democracy under Siege Too," *The Economist*, 17 July 2010.

56 In Great Britain, the liberal Yahad movement was established in late 2011. In Australia, the creation of a local branch of the New Israel Fund is fulfilling the same purpose.

57 For just one example, see David Chemla, *JCall: Les Raisons d'un Appel*, Paris: Liana Levi, 2011.

58 The Reut Institute, "Building a Political Firewall against Israel's Delegitimization," March 2010. Available at <www.reut-institute.org/data/uploads/PDFVer/20100310 Delegitimacy.Eng.pdf>.

59 Some of these points first appeared in Naomi Chazan, "Israeli Democracy and Identity under Attack," *Israel Studies Review*, vol. 26, no. 1, Summer 2011, 17–20.

6 Israel

The Shard in a Fragmenting Legal Order

Janice Gross Stein

The international legal order

Israel's conduct in war stands at the exposed shard of a fragmenting international legal order. Brought to attention recently by the Goldstone Report, Israel's conduct in an "asymmetrical war" raises all the contradictions of a legal order that is fragmenting, evolving, and yet, as flawed and incomplete as it is, critical to the legitimation of power and the use of force. Unfortunately, the Goldstone Report ignored all these complexities and contradictions and missed the chance to push forward the discussion of international law in a radically changed context.

Legal systems play an important role in constituting the structures of the worlds in which we live and in legitimating their practices. For the past three and a half centuries, the legal principle of sovereignty both reflected and shaped the international state system.

International legal orders are especially likely to lag behind the practices that they codify. They are inherently conservative, slow to change, deliberative in their style, and deliberate in their pace. International legal orders are especially slow to change because the opportunity for judgment and jurisprudence is, relatively speaking, so much less than in domestic legal systems. And, functionally, international legal orders evolve slowly because they are guarantors of institutional and practical legitimacy.

However, legal orders do change, as they incorporate new legal norms and principles. We need think only of the outlawing of genocide, a legal principle put in place after the Nazi genocide of the Jews in the Second World War, the prohibition of torture, the legal requirements in the treatment of prisoners-of-war, the adoption of the Geneva Conventions, the enshrinement of human rights in the international legal system, and the development of international humanitarian law—all changes to international law that occurred in the last century. Although some of these principles—and legal obligations—have often not been observed in practice, their legality is not contested. And insofar as their legality is not contested, they are the legitimating principles of the current international order.

A fragmenting legal order

The international legal order of the last three and a half centuries is, I want to argue, beginning to fracture, to slowly come apart. To focus on one among several dimensions, the constitutive principle of sovereignty is slowly coming undone. The doctrine of the Responsibility to Protect, for example, passed by the General Assembly of the United Nations in 2005, circumscribed the sovereignty of governments who systematically abuse their own citizens. The military intervention against the government of Muammar Gaddafi in the midst of an ongoing civil war in Libya was explicitly justified under Responsibility to Protect as an effort to prevent the imminent slaughter of tens of thousands of people in the city of Benghazi. Continuing air strikes targeted Gaddafi's artillery and armored vehicles that could have been used in attacks against the civilian population. Under carefully limited conditions, outside states can intervene—with force if genocide is imminent—to protect citizens from their abusive government. Sovereignty, and the consequent non-interference in the internal affairs of other states, no longer trumps all. It is now one among a series of legal principles which legitimate practice, and these principles can contradict one another. Unlike domestic legal orders, however, there is very little case law to help in the interpretation of these contradictions.

Nowhere are these contradictions more evident than in the conduct of war. What we call "asymmetrical war" is war which is unintelligible from the perspective of sovereignty as constitutive of the legal and political order. In asymmetrical war, at least one of the parties is an irregular force, representing no recognized sovereign state. The army has no uniform and the war has no front, no recognized battlefield. "By disguising themselves as civilians and by attacking civilians." argues Moshe Halbertal, a philosopher at the Hebrew University of Jerusalem who has worked closely with the Israel Defence Forces (IDF) on the role of ethics in war, non-state "organizations attempt nothing less than to erase the distinction between combatants and non-combatants on both sides of the struggle."[1]

Scholars mistake the meaning of asymmetrical war when they focus only on the asymmetries in military power. The critical difference here is not only an imbalance of military power, with one weaker and the other stronger. There are always imbalances of power in wars. The defining difference is that of form—one is a state, the other is not; one has an army, the other does not; and the front is everywhere and nowhere. The battlefield is among civilians, in neighborhoods, in streets, in cafés. In this kind of war, performance is often as important as material power and the contest is about legitimacy.

It is this kind of "asymmetrical war" that Israel has fought for the last two decades, on one front or another. It has fought these wars within a legal framework fraught with contradiction and ambiguity, because that legal framework was constructed within a framework of a war between states, between armies, in a defined battle space. That kind of war is now increasingly rare.

At least four sets of legal principles are at play:

- The laws of war, which have two separate sets of principles:
  - *Jus ad bellum*, or the legality of the war itself. Is the war just? Is it the last resort? Is there no other alternative? Here the law deals with the right to make war.[2]
  - *Jus in bello*, or the right conduct of war. The law focuses on practices, on what the combatants do to one another.
- The laws of human rights, which enshrine the universal right to life with dignity.
- International humanitarian law, which regulates the treatment of civilians in wartime and the humanitarian workers who provide assistance to populations at risk.

These four bodies of law, I argue, do not sit comfortably with one another and, at critical points, are in dynamic tension and contradiction with one another. The laws of war—which acknowledge that the use of force may be legitimate and right under some circumstances even when it leads to the death of an enemy warrior—are in full contradiction with human-rights law which accords every living being the right to life and dignity. There is no avoiding this contradiction: the laws of war supersede human-rights law as soon as a war is legitimated as just. It is difficult, therefore, to ground the laws of war in universal human rights.

Jus ad bellum, or just war theory, is not a legal code, which can be applied mechanically, but, as Michael Walzer argues in this volume, "a practice of systemic public reflection and argument, a shared vocabulary of ethical justifications and restraint." Leaders need to struggle with the question: Is the war necessary for self-defense? Could any other alternative protect the population? Or, given the nature of the threat, is war the only alternative? Is it the last resort?

Under any circumstances, this is an extraordinarily difficult question to answer. To do so, we need to rewind history and imagine alternative paths, roads that were not taken. It is especially hard to reimagine history in the context of asymmetrical warfare. In the days of state-to-state war, when one state attacked the territory of another, or its forces at sea, there was little ambiguity that the use of force in return in self-defense was just. However, when a militia sends its missiles against a civilian population, missiles which do no great physical damage, but nevertheless terrorize the population for months on end, is a use of force the only response? Has every other alternative been tried and failed? And is the firing of missiles against civilian populations itself an act of war, a *casus belli* that legitimates a use of force in response?

Few can answer these questions unambiguously, with assurance and confidence. It is for this reason that we debate the justness of war and pretend that we can measure justice along a continuum. Often we cannot and the world of asymmetric warfare is especially unforgiving. The first critical step is an affirmation of the justness of the use of force. It is the necessary precursor to any further discussion, for, if there is no right to make war, none of the remaining principles is material.

The laws of war and the UN Charter are unequivocal that governments have the right to self-defense when they are attacked. However, these laws were developed for state-to-state warfare, where attack is usually clear and unambiguous. There is no jurisprudence which sets out the parameters of attack in the asymmetrical context of a state and non-state actor, nor is there even rough agreement on threshold effects. How big does an attack by a non-state actor have to be? Does it matter whether infrastructure is disabled or people are killed? Did the attack by al-Qaeda on the World Trade Center cross the threshold? Why? Does that attack justify attacks against al-Qaeda's leaders, who are living in villages, attacks which simultaneously kill innocent civilians? Is pre-emptive assassination of known leaders who have perpetrated attacks in the past and may well do so again in the future a justifiable strategy under the laws of war? Or does there have to be credible evidence that a militant leader is planning an attack? Is that enough or does there have to be evidence that an attack is imminent? Was President Obama correct when he insisted that anyone who questioned the right of the United States to kill Osama bin Laden "had to have their head examined"? Who was acting as judge or jury and what guiding principle was the president using? Are strategies of targeted assassination against the leaders of groups committed to acts of terror against civilians just? All these questions are now being debated not only by philosophers and lawyers, but also by lawyers trained in the laws of war and embedded in fighting units. These are practical as well as ethical and legal questions that are being adjudicated first on the ground, through practice, by armies fighting asymmetrical wars.

Historical context is often determining. In the period preceding Israel's attack against Hamas, in January 2006, it imposed a blockade after Hamas became the government in Gaza. A blockade is generally considered an act of war in international law. In June 2006, Hamas militants crossed the border, killed two of Israel's soldiers and kidnapped a third. Within days, a five-month shooting war erupted, followed by sporadic firing of rockets and retaliation by Israel. It was not until June 2008 that Egypt mediated a six-month truce where Hamas agreed not to fire rockets and Israel agreed to refrain from the targeting of Hamas leaders and offices and to reopen all but the Rafah crossing into Gaza under appropriate international supervision. Although the expected prisoner exchange did not materialize, the truce held until November when attacks across the border escalated again. Israel then launched an all-out attack against Hamas forces in Gaza. The attack was not designed to destroy Hamas—it was not a war of regime change—but rather to compel Hamas to cease firing rockets at Israel's civilian populations. Strategies of compellence work by raising the costs—directly or indirectly—to leaders so that they desist from unwanted action.

Was the attack just? There are often no unequivocal answers to this question, in part because of the chain of historical events. In this case, Israel's blockade, legally an act of war, preceded Hamas' firing of rockets. Unquestionably, Hamas then fired rockets at Israel's civilians, which terrorized the population and occasionally killed innocent civilians. Firing of rockets is unmistakably an act of war, which in turn legitimates the use of force in self-defense. These rocket attacks were not an existential threat to the survival of Israel, however, and indeed Israel allowed them to continue for two years, before finally resorting to the use of force in order to defend its civilians and compel Hamas to cease firing.

This was the context in which the Goldstone Report had the opportunity to reopen the larger questions of the justness of war in asymmetrical warfare. Justice Richard Goldstone was asked by the United Nations Human Rights Council to head a fact-finding mission on the legality of the war in Gaza and the behavior of both combatants, Israel and Hamas. After lengthy negotiation on the mandate of the Mission, members travelled to Gaza to interview civilians who had been harmed during the war and relatives of those who had been killed. Israel refused to cooperate officially with the Mission, arguing that the Human Rights Council had a long record of bias against Israel. The Goldstone Report, made public on 15 September 2009, unfortunately missed the opportunity to interrogate the relevance of international law to asymmetric conflict and to examine where the laws had to be supple in application, even though its principles held. The Report paid far more attention to right conduct in war than it did to the prior question of the justness of the war.

The Goldstone Report left unanswered the broad question of whether there are any conditions when non-state actors are justified in attacking the civilian infrastructure of an adversarial state. The Commission answered only partially and indirectly by finding evidence of potential war crimes and "possible crimes against humanity" by both Israel and Hamas. "That the crimes allegedly committed by Hamas were intentional," Goldberg subsequently explained, "goes without saying—its rockets were purposefully and indiscriminately aimed at civilian targets."[3] The intentional striking of civilians is unjust and, by implication, legitimates a use of force in response. The question for Israel, and for others, who fight asymmetrical wars, is: What constitutes a legal and a just response? The two are not always the same.

The Report is clear that international law applies as much to asymmetric conflict as it does to inter-state war: "Simply put," argued Goldstone,

> the laws of armed conflict apply no less to non-state actors such as Hamas than they do to national armies. Ensuring that non-state actors respect these principles, and are investigated when they fail to do so, is one of the most significant challenges facing the law of armed conflict. Only if all parties to armed conflict are held to these standards will we be able to protect civilians who, through no choice of their own, are caught up in war.[4]

This preliminary judgment suggests that no deliberate attack against civilians can be justified, whether by a state or a non-state actor. If this judgment, which has yet to be litigated or codified, stands, it would remove the most effective strategy that weaker non-state actors use against stronger states that they seek to wear down and exhaust through attrition. It would unmistakably consider as illegal any acts of terror launched against civilians and it would make those who use such strategies subject to international arrest and prosecution by the International Criminal Court.

The issues around *jus in bello*, the legality of the practices of war, are even more challenging. What constitutes a just military response to attacks by non-state actors against civilians? Israel had repeatedly warned against the attacks, threatened consequences, and responded with raids, but Hamas was unde-terred. The attacks continued. Israel's leaders knew full well that a military response, no matter how carefully planned, no matter how surgically designed, would inevitably kill far more civilians than the Hamas rockets had because of the density of the population in Gaza and the emplacement of Hamas fighters among the civilian populations. Even with no deliberate intention to kill civilians, even if civilians were warned in advance of impending attacks, large numbers of civilians would be killed as Hamas placed mobile rocket launchers in the midst of civilians, as fighters were embedded in communities. In the context of asymmetric warfare, how do leaders of the state do this calculus of self-defense? How do the laws of war speak to this radically different context? Unfortunately, the Goldstone Report is fatally silent about how context moderates legal principles, yet it is context that is at the core of the application of law to cases.

Moshe Halbertal wrestled precisely with this issue in his critical review of the Goldstone Report. Some argue, he says, that:

> since such a struggle necessarily involves the killing of innocent civilians, there is no justifiable way of fighting it. Soldiers ought to refuse to engage in such a war, and the government has only one option, which is to end the occupation. This view is wrong, since Israel has the right and the obligation to protect its citizens, and without providing real security, it will fail also to achieve peace and to put an end to the occupation. [Others] claim that, since Hamas and Hezbollah initiated the targeting of Israeli civilians, and since they take refuge among their own civilians, the responsibility for harming Palestinian civilians during Israel's attempt to defend itself falls upon the Palestinians exclusively. This approach is also wrong. The killing of our civilians does not justify the killing of their civilians. Civilians do not lose their right to life when they are used as shields by Hamas and Hezbollah. In fighting the militants, Israel must do as much as it possibly can do to avoid and minimize harm to civilian life and property.[5]

Halbertal argues, as does Michael Walzer, that it is not enough to refrain from intentionally harming civilians. A state must take positive steps to avoid harming civilians. What does this mean in practice? How do commanders make these judgments? Do they put the safety of their soldiers first, before the safety of the civilian populations? This is a vexing judgment, usually made in a split second, when militia fighters are embedded among civilian populations. International law and legitimacy, I shall argue, are part of the stakes in asymmetric warfare.

Practices in asymmetric war

Jus in bello, laws governing the conduct of war, have been the overwhelming focus of controversy in asymmetric war. These laws, developed over the centuries but sharpened and refined during the classic state system of the Westphalian period, were developed for war between states, with armies, in a defined battle space. How well can these laws be applied to asymmetric wars that are fought between states and non-state actors, with differing kinds and levels of military capabilities? Not only are the types of participants in asymmetric wars different, but also the battle space has changed. Fighting is not confined within bounded space; asymmetric wars are fought in jungles, in streets, in refugee camps, but, most importantly, in the midst of population centers. The forces that non-state actors deploy are often quite deliberately embedded within population centers so that the population shields and protects the fighters. Guns and anti-aircraft rockets are intentionally placed on the rooftops of apartment buildings so that an attack on these gun emplacements will almost certainly cause civilian casualties.

One way of thinking about the strategy of asymmetric warfare is to see it as a deliberate attempt by the non-state actor that is almost always weaker to mobilize international legal norms as a resource in the larger struggle. By provoking the adversary to violate norms and rules of international law, it helps to delegitimize the state in the broader international community. The goal is to create a pariah state, outside the boundaries of the international community.

Why then does the state respond to what is a deliberate provocation? Why is it ensnared by what is an obvious trap? For the state in the asymmetric war, doing nothing imposes high costs. Its own population feels vulnerable and unprotected and the pressure grows on political leaders over time. The state loses legitimacy with its own citizens if it allows attacks against its own civilians to go unpunished. It is this legitimacy trap which makes asymmetric warfare so treacherous for the state: if it responds, it risks the loss of international legitimacy but, if it does not respond, it risks the loss of domestic legitimacy.

There is a second dilemma for the state involved in asymmetric warfare. It may not respond because it is deterred by the risk of injuring or killing innocent civilians and violating international law. If it does nothing, however, it risks encouraging its adversary to escalate, to push harder because the objective is indeed to provoke a response. The logic is unforgiving: a failure to respond is likely to provoke escalation and compromise deterrence, but response is likely to kill or injure civilians and provoke international condemnation and delegitimization. For those who confront the dilemmas of response, as Emanuel Adler has put it in another context, damned if you do and damned if you don't.

International law sets out several criteria which govern the use of force in wartime. Four are particularly important and often misunderstood: distinction, proportionality, necessity, and avoidance. These four principles shape the practices of those states that seek a legal and legitimate response in asymmetrical warfare.

The principle of distinction absolutely prohibits the intentional targeting of noncombatants. This becomes very difficult in asymmetrical war, where combatants wear no uniforms and are embedded among civilians.

- Can you intentionally target militia members who live in crowded neighborhoods?
- Can you target the financier of an operation designed to explode bombs among your civilians? Are those who trained the would-be bombers in New York legitimate targets?
- Is targeted assassination, the policy followed by Israel and now by the United States in Pakistan, legitimate? On what grounds? On prevention of attack? Who "judges" the strength of the incriminating evidence before such a strike is launched? If the leaders who have ordered attacks against civilians live in law-abiding societies, where the rule of law prevails and arrest, detention, and a fair trial are likely, then assassination is not legitimate. If they do not, such an action may be legal, but not necessarily just, argues Michael Walzer.[6]

A second principle, proportionality, is badly understood by the public and the media and extraordinarily difficult to apply in practice. Counter to our intuition, proportionality does not refer to a balance in casualties among the warring parties. If 100 Afghans and 10 Canadians are dead after an operation, that asymmetrical balance does not establish the absence of proportionality. In the war against Hamas, Israel lost 10 soldiers and 3 civilians, while Gazans, according to some estimates, suffered 1,285 dead, of whom approximately one-third were civilians. This dramatically lopsided outcome does not, however, establish that Israel's response to Hamas' firing of rockets was disproportionate. Proportionality is not about the numbers who are killed, or even about the numbers of civilians killed. As Justice Goldstone argued, "That comparatively few Israelis have been killed by the unlawful rocket and mortar attacks from Gaza in no way minimizes the criminality [of the rocket attacks]."[7] War crimes hinge on intentions, not on outcomes.

Proportionality applies when it is likely that civilians will be killed as a result of the use of force. The principle of proportionality requires that the death of civilians be proportionate to the military advantage that will be achieved by eliminating the target.[8] This is an extraordinarily complex principle to apply in practice. "Is the potential risk to civilians excessive in relationship to the anticipated military advantage?" asked one observer.

> That puts the weight on military advantage, since civilian risk is a given and must not be "excessive." Even if the target is legitimate, was the right weapon used to try to minimize civilian damage? The key is the expected damage the commander anticipated from the use of a certain weapon, and not what actually happened when it was fired.[9]

It goes without saying that the scope for subjectivity in these kinds of judgments is enormous. How do commanders weigh military advantage in practice? How great a weight do they give to the safety of their own soldiers as they advance through a neighborhood when snipers are hiding in buildings and how do they weigh that safety against the safety of civilians? These are truly Hobson's choices.

What do the IDF do in practice to grapple with these kinds of dilemmas? The IDF created an International Law Division (DABLA) and, drawing on the expertise of philosophers in the universities, reviewed the laws of war as they apply to asymmetric warfare and targeted assassination to provide guidelines for commanders. DABLA personnel provided advice to the General Staff in the planning of the attack, were embedded with the troops, and attended operational meetings.

The distinction between civilians and combatants was often very difficult, if not impossible, to make, since Hamas fighters generally fought without uniforms. If commanders are unable to make that distinction, they are consequently unable to make informed judgments about proportionality. Nevertheless, officers are told that the distinction between combatants and civilian targets needs to be made, no matter how difficult. Avichai Mandelblit, the Israeli Military Advocate General, elaborated on the practical responsibilities of jurists at the operational level:

> A military jurist, like any legal adviser, is obliged to give the body he is advising the whole gamut of legal tools to achieve its goals while strictly adhering to the law ... It reflects our professional understanding that the commanders need legal advisers who are accessible and trained, who will point out what is forbidden and permitted. Legal advice with regard to operative decisions is not theoretical or academic. It is expressed in the commanders' far-reaching decisions. There is no place in this kind of advice for the vague and non-binding style that sometimes typifies academic thinking and writing. Like the commanders, the military legal advisers are required to formulate clear positions and opinions in real time, amid the fog of battle, in circumstances that heighten the legal dilemmas that characterize modern warfare.[10]

These are admirable instructions that are very difficult to follow in practice. What kind of advice do military jurists provide when eliminating the leader of an operation that will kill 200 civilians is likely to cause the death of 30 civilians? Even when there is very good information, how do military jurists make this judgment of proportionality? What criteria of proportionality should be used is not made clear in the law. Philosophers answer only that positive efforts must be made to limit the harm to civilians.

The third and fourth principles are necessity and avoidance. These two principles are in tension with one another, as well as with some of the other principles of international law. Necessity requires that the least amount of force possible be used to accomplish the mission. In conventional war, it is easier, though by no means easy, to gauge the amount of force that is necessary to accomplish an objective. In asymmetrical war, it is far more uncertain, given the mobility of the targets and the fluidity of the battle. If a militia leader is travelling in a convoy, what is the minimum amount of force necessary to attack the single car and not injure anyone else in the convoy?

But even this principle comes into conflict with the principle of avoidance. Soldiers are obligated, as we have seen, to do their utmost to avoid harm to innocent civilians. The tension between these two principles is clear: to return to the militia leader travelling in the car, is it permissible to strike the car if the militia leader's family is riding with him but he is travelling on a deserted highway? Or must the attack wait until he is alone in the car, but with no assurance that he will not likely again be on a deserted highway? Is it only permissible to attack if there is concrete evidence that he is planning an attack? Is it permissible to do so if he has ordered attacks in the past? These are not theoretical issues but practical conundrums which the Obama administration faced when they received confirming evidence that Osama bin Laden was hiding in a walled-off compound. They had no good information about how many civilians and family members were in the compound with him. Nor did they have concrete evidence of an impending attack. The principles of proportionality, necessity, and avoidance were all in play in this decision, but without specific guidelines.

Many of these judgments are in tension with one another and any recognition of the necessity—and the justice—of the use of force is in tension with the fundamental principles of human rights. These tensions are exacerbated by the decline of sovereignty as the constitutive principle of international life and the growing prominence of asymmetric war in our changing world. These judgments often—though not always—conflict with the military imperative to do the utmost to protect the lives of one's soldiers. In an age of asymmetric warfare, it is at best a judgment of reasonable and practical men and women, fully informed of their ethical and legal obligations, who grapple with their responsibilities to their own soldiers that they put in harm's way, to their citizens, and to civilians everywhere.

Epilogue: Justice reconsidered

The Goldstone Report accused both Israel and Hamas of potential war crimes and "possibly crimes against humanity," but the Report paid overwhelming attention to Israel. "In reviewing the incidents," the Report concluded, "the mission found in every case that the Israeli armed forces had carried out direct intentional strikes against civilians." It was the intentionality of the use of force against civilians that the Goldstone Report considered as definitive. The Goldstone Mission demanded that Israel—as well as Hamas—investigate these incidents before it made its final recommendations. This judgment of deliberate intention was somewhat surprising since Israel had refused to cooperate with the Mission and therefore the commissioners heard no direct testimony about intentionality.

Then came the stunning admission by Justice Goldstone, in an op-ed he published on 1 April 2011, 18 months after the publication of the Report:

> We know a lot more today about what happened in the Gaza war of 2008–09 than we did when I chaired the fact-finding mission. If I had known then what I know now, the Goldstone Report would have been a different document.[11]

What did Goldstone learn in the intervening year? Hamas had conducted no investigations of its alleged war crimes, while Israel had launched more than 400 operational investigations. An independent review of these investigations found some misconduct by individual soldiers but concluded that "civilians were not intentionally targeted as a matter of policy." Even though the investigations were conducted by Israel's officials, the principal ground on which the Goldstone Report had alleged war crimes no longer appeared to be valid.

Even when the intentions of the state and the stronger party are no longer at issue, *jus in bello*, or its practices in war, as well as those of the weaker, non-state actor, remain challenging in asymmetric warfare. First, Justice Goldstone argued, the laws of war do apply to asymmetric war. "I continue to believe," he insisted,

> in the cause of establishing and applying international law to protracted and deadly conflicts. Simply put, the laws of armed conflict apply no less to non-state actors like Hamas than they do to national armies. Only if all parties to armed conflicts are held to these standards will we be able to protect civilians who, through no choice of their own, are caught up in war.[12]

Yet the Report made no systematic effort to come to grips with the challenge of protecting civilians when neighborhoods and streets are the battlegrounds, when militias use civilians as human shields, when guns are on the roofs of residences, and when one side deliberately provokes the other to fire on civilians.

The Goldstone Report missed a historic opportunity to explore new legalities as the existing order fragments. Laws command respect only so long as they speak to the dilemmas of their times and, unfortunately, the laws of war no longer do. In this sense, Israel is the shard of a fragmenting legal order; in its wars, it exposes the inadequacies of the existing global corpus of the laws of war, a body of law developed for wars no longer fought and silent on many of the issues in the wars that are fought.

Why then—in the midst of war—struggle with these legal principles and judgments? Why then—in the face of an enemy—take any risk at all with a soldier's life? We return, as Michael Walzer argued, to "a practice of systemic public reflection and argument, a shared vocabulary of ethical justifications and restraint." We do so in part for instrumental reasons and in part because the way societies fight wars shapes who they are and how they see themselves. In asymmetrical war, legitimacy is especially important. The purpose of asymmetrical war is often to delegitimize the other, to force it to behave in ways that are generally considered illegitimate and less than fully human. Once we understood that asymmetric war is a struggle for legitimacy, it becomes clear why struggling with the ethical imperatives of the laws of war matters, and matters a great deal. This struggle, moreover, is important not only for instrumental reasons—to avoid delegitimization—but also for the values and the identity of a society facing the challenge.

How will this struggle take place? In asymmetric ways. Some societies are engaging actively with the reinterpretation of the laws of war. They are doing so as a matter of practice, by embedding military jurists with local commanders who advise on decisions on the ground in the heat of combat, and by refining legal abstractions in the face of the unforgiving realities of combat. That has been the recent experience of the IDF, as well as other armies that face the challenges of asymmetrical warfare. That they are so engaged is encouraging, because, as I have argued, it is through practice that a new legal order will emerge. Through this struggle, the content of international laws of war will be redefined and remade for the twenty-first century.

Notes

1 Moshe Halbertal, "The Goldstone Illusion," *The New Republic*, 6 November 2009.
2 For modern discussions of this traditional distinction, see the seminal work by Michael Walzer, *Just and Unjust Wars*, New York: Basic Books, 1977, pp. 21–47.
3 Richard Goldstone, "Reconsidering the Goldstone Report on Israel and War Crimes," *The Washington Post*, 1 April 2011. Available at <http://www.washington post.com/opinions/reconsidering-the-goldstone-report-on-israel-and-war-crimes/2011/04/01/AFg111JC_story.html>.
4 Ibid.
5 Halbertal, "The Goldstone Illusion."
6 Cited by A. Harel, "Goldstone Report Failed to Address Difficulties of Asymmetric Warfare," *Haaretz*, 18 May 2011.
7 Goldstone, "Reconsidering the Goldstone Report on Israel and War Crimes."
8 For a discussion of the different meanings of proportionality, see Lionel Beehmer, "Israel and the Doctrine of Proportionality," *Report for the Council of Foreign Relations*, 13 July 2006. See also Thomas Hurka, "Proportionality in the Morality of War," *Philosophy and Public Affairs,* vol. 33, no. 1, 2005, 34–66.
9 Steven Erlanger, "Weighing Crimes and Ethics in the Fog of Urban Warfare," *New York Times*, 16 January 2009.

10 Avichai Mandelblit, "Advice under Fire," *Haaretz*, 29 January 2009, cited by Howard Adelman, "Intent: *Jus in Bello* Norms in Just War Theory: The Case of the War in Gaza in 2009," paper presented to the annual meeting of the International Studies Association, 15 February 2009, New York. See also Howard Adelman, "The War between Two Conflicting Ethical Systems: Just War Ethics versus Human Right," paper presented to the annual meeting of the Israel Studies Association, 10 May 2010, Toronto, ON.

11 Goldstone, "Reconsidering the Goldstone Report on Israel and War Crimes."

12 Ibid., p. 2.

7 Four States, Two People, One Solution
Can Israel Maintain Its Identity?

Zvi Bar'el

Borders or a nation

Three very simple questions are bothering me lately:

- How many states can one people have?
- In how many states can a person establish his identity?
- Where is the Israeli identity located?

Normal people with regular problems are not as lucky as we, Israelis, are. We are the *Chosen People*, true, but we were also given too many options to choose from. One example is our homeland. There is the biblical Eretz Israel, which would include Jordan, Egypt, and Iraq of today. There is also Israel of the partition plan; Israel of the Green Line; the Blue Line; the Purple Line—with the Golan Heights—and Israel with East Jerusalem, and without it. We have Israel with its branches in the West Bank, and we have an Israeli Diaspora, not in the United States but in Hebron, Ofra, and Efrat, where some 350,000 people, about 5 percent of the state's population, are living. We have an imagined Israel, where most of the Israeli population has not stepped a foot in, and we have the real Israel, the state which was recognized by the international community.

No wonder that we are confused, no wonder that we have chosen our government according to our dreams, but realize that we bought ourselves a nightmare.

We should be thankful to our Palestinian neighbors who are in the same position. They also have too many states to choose from. They too have Eretz Palestine, which had nourished their dreams; they have Palestine of the partition plan; the occupied Palestine; Palestine minus settlements; and Palestine with Gaza and without Gaza—in short, they, like us, are not just Chosen People. They, like us, are the *Choosing People*, people who are always in the process of choosing the right place for their homeland, for their identity.

Israelis are not unique in that situation, but we have a special feature in our identity complex. We draw our identity from our inner-Diaspora, from the settlers. Like the Palestinians whose national purpose is to create a state for their refugees, Israel has identified itself as a shelter. However, in the last 45 years, Israel went through an additional phase. Israel has become subjugated to the settlers' state to such an extent that its future and its aim as a state are subjected to its ability to *sell* its new borders and its new territorial identity not to the world but to the settlers. In other words, the settlers are bestowed with the authority to define the nature and the identity of the State of Israel. "Borders are also meaning-making and meaning-carrying entities. Parts of cultural landscapes which often transcend the physical limits of the state and defy the power of state institutions," Hastings and Wilson wrote wisely.[1] However, in the Israeli case, it is difficult to define the location of the state's cultural borders, and the identity of the "meaning-makers" who dwell beyond its physical borders.

It is almost impossible now to relate to Israel as a nation-state, as Ulrich Beck, Eric Hobsbawm, Benedict Anderson, or Clifford Geertz (1973)[2] had tried to define the term. Interestingly, Israel's relations with the settlers call for a revision of Anderson's theory about Imagined Communities, since the Motherland became the imitator rather than the object of imitation. Contrary to most cultural and political theories, hegemony in Israel shifts from the governing elite to a minority inner-Diaspora.

The Goddess of security

This identity clash had begun with the initial euphoria of the grand victory in 1967 and a messianic idea that engulfed it.[3] It went on through a short clashing period between the settlers and a confused state, a state that until 1977 perceived the occupied territories to be a mere deposit, or a negotiating card, which should be handed back to Jordan and Syria once peace is achieved.[4] This was the period when the term *benevolent occupation* was embedded in the Israeli discourse and the ideological discourse had just started to form the *correct* language for the outcome of the war: should it be called an occupation or is it the beginning of the salvation, *Geula*?

However, even those who adopted the term *freed territories* as opposed to *occupied territories*, and those who became the first settlers, had to derive their identity from that of the State of Israel.

Security reasons, coined by Igal Alon and others, were adopted as a rationale for establishing the settlements. Security for the State of Israel then meant that the settlements would be part of Israel's security defense line. This *civil wall* was to absorb the first possible attack by any enemy coming from the East.[5]

One should not be too serious in analyzing the military logic behind that argument. Questions such as how exactly the settlements were supposed to protect the State of Israel against foreign attacks and whether they would become a burden on the army in time of war were never seriously discussed. Suffice it to remember that most settlements in the West Bank and in the Golan Heights were evacuated once the Yom Kippur War broke out.

Yet the security pretext remained, serving two purposes: confiscation of lands for *security reasons*, and granting the settlers and the settlements with a proper Israeli aura and legitimacy. That is, the settlers are not just squatters, nor are they messianic enthusiasts; they are at the service of the state, civil soldiers, who are ready to sacrifice their comfort for the security of the state.[6]

The Goddess of security did not have to invest too much of an effort to convince the Israeli public that the settlers are in her service. They looked like soldiers, they adopted military tasks, and they have retaliated against what they have perceived as Palestinian *misbehavior*. In fact, they have exchanged roles with the army. The settlers stepped in where the army could not operate because of its perception of its duty to serve the Palestinian population. Thus, for example, when the army tried to maintain the religious status quo in the Tomb of the Patriarchs in Hebron, the settlers of Kiryat Arba managed to shatter the delicate balance and to change the division line between Jewish and Muslim prayers, which has been carefully kept for years. By the end of the 1970s, they settled in the Jewish quarter of Hebron, causing the evacuation of many Palestinian families, blocking the main street of the city, and operating as the proprietors of the city. This had nothing to do with security; it was aimed at turning the imagined Jewish narrative into a new reality; to put the city of the ancestors back into the hands of Jews and to establish it as part of the present, rather than leaving it as part of its legendary biblical past.

Places and monuments that were serving the nation's dreams as part of its identity, chapters in the ancient past that were feeding the collective memory, received new tasks in the nation's life: they became a tool for a geographical identity of the nation. This newly designed territorial identity, according to the settlers, should justify the next stage: the popular identity, where the *empty space* dotted by holy places will become an essential part of the state's present and future identity. Hence, not culture, tradition or any other historical contents were to define Israeli identity, but extended territory that uses past icons as political rather than religious or cultural identifiers.

The army and the state had to follow suit. It was no longer the case of people returning to their ancient country; rather, it was convincing the Israeli state that, without controlling and settling in the ancient country, the Motherland and its people would lose their identity. This is the phase when borders and international laws cease to draw the line between Israel and its occupied territories and a new map of identification becomes the order of the day.

According to this new map, there is an *Israeli space* and a *Jewish space*. While the Israeli space characterizes the citizens of Israel, Jews and Arabs, and symbolizes the positive law, and the internationally recognized Israel as a member of the community of nations, the Jewish space knows no such borders and no such characteristics. The Jewish space took it upon itself to supply the Israeli space with its spiritual content: a new cocktail of nationalism and religion blended with messianic enthusiasm, which is to become the new litmus test for the *real Israeli*.

Dressing identity with the law

The Israeli civil-military complex in the occupied territories could not remain fluid; it had to be constructed formally in order to avoid a situation of *no land's citizens*. Hence, by the beginning of the 1980s, it was no longer a rope-pulling competition between the army (or the state for that matter) and the settlers; a new process had begun. This was the time when the settlers became a class rather than an enclave society. The difference between the two terms is, *inter alia*, that an enclave does not strive to set an example for the whole society, but it needs the protection of the law in order to maintain its status as enclave.[7] A class, on the other hand, especially an elite class, puts forward its demands from the greater society, and demands respect and recognition, which could be provided by law or by practice. The cultural practice, which aims at establishing the settlers as elite, was not there yet; this will come later.

Nevertheless, the State of Israel stepped in by granting the settlers both: they became a symbol of new Zionism, latter-day heroes, and they were given formal recognition as part of Israel by enforcing the Israeli law over the settlements without officially annexing them to the state.[8]

Building new settlements, developing infrastructure, mapping new borders for already existing settlements, and drawing plans for enlarging them then became an act of the state and no longer the result of yielding to pressures and illegal acts of the settlers. By cladding the settlements with a legal dress, the settlers were not just protected, they also became official partners of the state, thus imposing on the state an obligation to accept its out-of-the-state citizens as part of its body politic. Now it was time to establish the cultural adoption of the settlers.

A few years ago, the settlers realized that their major problem was that they were perceived as outsiders and not as Israelis, people who are part of an endangered Diaspora and who have the option to return to safe Israel. Some articles in the press even suggested that a settler who is a victim of a terror attack should be less important than an Israeli victim should.[9] As if settlers' blood is cheaper than Israeli blood. As a response to that attitude, the settlers started a campaign that carried the slogan "to settle in the hearts of Israelis." Another slogan stated, "Yesha is here," meaning that Judea and Samaria are inside Israel. If they are in danger, so is Israel.[10]

A few years later, those slogans were abandoned. There was no need for them anymore. Paraphrasing on the settlers' slogan, Israel finds itself bound to settle in the settlers' hearts. To tell them that Tel Aviv or Kfar Saba are in Judea and Samaria, that we are one state. In other words, the raison d'être of Israel is to protect the existence of the settlements.

That is where the fundamental paradox became a reality. The *mother-state* became a servant state.

A satellite state

"Not all of the settlers are Teitels," shouted the settlers from their bunkers. Referring to the case of ultra-orthodox Jewish extremist Jacob Teitel, an immigrant from the United States charged with multiple hate crimes, including the murder of an Arab shepherd and taxi driver in 1997 and the planting of an explosive device at the front door of a family of Messianic Jews in Ariel that seriously injured 15-year-old Ami Ortiz. "We must not smear an entire community because of one killer," chanted their chorus, closing ranks whenever one of "their own," alone or in collaboration, a killer or a *hilltop-youth*, deviates from the rules of the game.

They are right. The *pure camp* of the settlers must not be *infected* by the likes of Baruch Goldstein, by the Bat Ayin underground, by Jewish provocation in Hebron's Avraham Avinu neighborhood, by the *freedom fighters* on the hilltops. Like any nation, the settlers' nation has its deviants, terrorists, and murderers, and even homosexuals, God forbid. This is a nation like any other. The polemic over the question of settlers' responsibility for the criminals among them, in the best case, is irrelevant and, in the worst, obfuscates their real sin.

The settlers' crime lies not in raising murderers, or even in nurturing a culture of hate toward the Palestinians or scorn for the Tel Aviv *bubble*. Their sin is in their settlement itself. They are not simply building homes and tending gardens, real-estate mavens taking advantage of the good deal afforded by the Six-Day War. Rather, they chose to create a separate nation, and established one with its own territory, laws, language, ideology, and customs. It is a nation that conducts foreign policy with the State of Israel, with its own law-enforcement agency and militias to strike anyone threatening its borders. It has efficient intelligence whose agents work within Israel's government and army, and its own public-relations apparatus.

The settlers have turned the State of Israel into their satellite. Their power is so great that even a superpower like the United States caves in against their obstinacy. What do they care about peace with the Palestinians or Syria, the Arab peace initiative or the Iranian nuclear threat? A house in Ofra, a neighborhood in Efrat, a trailer home in Givat Rachel are far more important to them than the fate of the Israeli *bubble*, which in its stupidity knows not where its peace process is truly leading.

The fact that Israel Defense Forces brigades were forced to cancel exercises in order to protect them, and the enormous cost of guaranteeing their security, creating such strong opposition in Israel that even Ariel Sharon, their erstwhile prince, decided to end their costly adventure in Gaza and remove the settlers from the Gaza Strip did not bother them. In the settler narrative, which has succeeded in taking root in Israel, that reason for the disengagement from the Gaza Strip has disappeared.

Now Yaakov "Jack" Teitel has come to their aid. He is not *all* of the settlers, but he is the decoy whose role was to divert the discourse away from the settlers and the strategic threat that they represent, onto various criminological and sociological polemics over whether it is a person's environment or DNA that turns him into an assassin. A fair question indeed, but irrelevant. Teitels do not have to be settlers in order to kill those who don't agree with their views.

The State of Israel will not live or die over such an assassin, or a dozen more like him. The country is engaged in a national struggle with the settlers' state. If there is a strategic threat to Israel's continued survival, it sits on the hills of Hebron and Samaria. If there is one force that can bring down the continuation of the peace process, it is the continued building in the settlements. If the US ultimately chooses to cut Israel off, it will be because of the settlements not because of Teitels.

Across the Green Line there are two states, Palestinian and Jewish, which do not see eye to eye with the State of Israel. While the Palestinian state has a chance to reach peace with Israel, the settlers' state sees Israel as a strategic threat and its leadership as a gang of ditherers, a state threatening to undermine the power of the settlers' state. In their eyes, Israel is the real exile, dancing to the tune of a corrupt American overlord.

The roles have reversed. No longer are settlers seeking to settle in the hearts of Israelis; they are putting forth an unequivocal demand that Israelis inhabit the settlers' hearts—or else.

Therefore, the question is not whether Israel is an occupying state in the West Bank and East Jerusalem, rather, where are the boundaries of the Israeli identity. Hence, we consider the Palestinians not just enemies of *old Israel* but also a threat to the Israeli national identity. It is not just an Israeli longing for the biblical Promised Land that drives Israel's policies, or defining the tomb of Abraham in Hebron and that of Rachel in Bethlehem as historic heritage; it is the fear of losing the identity that nourishes Israel's conflict with the Palestinians. This fear stretches out to the extent that the state feels obliged to safeguard every outpost that has been built in the occupied territories, legally or illegally, while the legality of their status stems not from international recognition but from their symbolic value. Those outposts turned out to be small capsules of the state. Thus, Obama's demand to freeze the building in the settlements is perceived as infringing on Israel's sovereignty not as an occupier but as an owner. Yet again, this is not just a political and a strategic dispute between Israel and the US, it is about cultural definitions.

Where is the State of Israel?

I do not know how to calculate the life span of a generation in Israel, yet my students would probably be considered the second generation after the 1967 war. They are in their twenties, born into the second phase of the occupation. They were not part of the Israeli euphoria, most of them had their *after army* trip to all kinds of remote corners of the world, and most of them never stepped foot beyond the Green Line. However, when I would ask them where Ofra is or where Kdumim is, they would rarely be able to point to these places on the map; nevertheless, they are sure that these places are inside Israel. The settlers' plan has succeeded completely. They no longer need to settle in the hearts and minds of young Israelis to convince them that Yesha "is here" inside Israel. Israel has become part of Yesha.

The interesting thing is to watch Israeli protesters who try to defend Palestinian farmers, who are prevented by settlers, many times violently, from cultivating their lands or harvesting their crops. Their protest is not against the actual building of settlements; they are just trying to establish better conditions for the Palestinians under the occupation. As if to say "if the occupation is inevitable, let's make it more tolerable." Paradoxically, the claim to enhance human-rights conditions in the occupied territories is tantamount to a call to return to the *benevolent occupation*, a slogan that shaped the first years of the occupation. Such is also the condemnation of the apartheid reality in the West Bank. There is no apartheid in the occupied territories—it is an occupation regime with all the ugliness, misbehavior, violence, and abuse that characterizes any occupation. However, when Israel applies the Israeli law on its settlers in the West Bank, it seems just fair to demand the same application of the Israeli law on the Palestinians.

Two Palestinian states

Israelis are not the only people who by now have two states. Our neighbors the Palestinians have the same problem. They too have two states, one in Gaza and one in the West Bank and East Jerusalem. They too have no final borders yet, and, like the Israelis, they are in search of their territory that will define their nation. While their identity as people is more or less crystallized, their transformation from a people into a defined and sovereign state reflects a dual complexity.

The Palestinians have to solve their ideological and political problems with Hamas and they have to reconcile with their historical dreams. It is not just the question of who will rule Gaza and how the national budget and major governmental posts would be divided between Hamas and Fatah. It has to do with the character of the future state. Will it be religious? What kind of curriculum will be taught at schools? Will it be another Iraq? Another Turkey, or perhaps a second Saudi Arabia?

Practically, the division between Gaza and the West Bank poses an historic dilemma for the Palestinian authority. It consists of two fundamental questions: first, if there is no agreement as to the nature of the state, will the Palestinian authority be willing to establish a state without Gaza? The answer to that is no. The Palestinian authority cannot and will not detach itself from 1.5 million Palestinians in Gaza. It will have to find a political compromise with Hamas even if it may hinder any peace settlement with Israel.[11]

Second, if there is an agreement on the nature of the state and Hamas will become an integral part of it, what will be its relations with Israel?

So far, there are inherent contradictions between an internal Palestinian reconciliation and recognition of the State of Israel, mainly because Hamas refuses to recognize Israel, and, without recognizing Israel, even the Palestinian authority finds it impossible to come to terms with Hamas. It is not because the Palestinians share the Israeli agenda, far from it, but because they had adopted long ago the idea that recognition is part of their privilege and power. In fact, the Palestinians need Israel's recognition—before any other state—of their independent state. Without recognizing the State of Israel first, their demand for recognition from a *non-state* has no meaning.

On the other hand, it is quite odd to see how the State of Israel is seeking recognition from a non-state entity, and how the Palestinian authority was eager to grant it as part of its self-recognition. Hamas is not there yet, as Hamas does not consider itself as a state authority but rather an opposition with territory, which is part of the Palestinian state.

With all differences considered, Hamas behaves like the settlers. Both want their Motherland to adapt to their ideology, both consider their primary state to be a menace to their national vision, yet both do not want to detach completely from their primary state. In fact, Hamas and the settlers prefer the "four-states" situation to the two-states solution.

More importantly, Hamas and the settlers maintain enough power to prevent the two-states solution by posing the crucial question: which Israeli state should the Palestinian authority recognize? If, for the sake of argument, the Palestinian authority (with Hamas) recognizes the State of Israel as a Jewish state, it, inherently, has to recognize the fact that that state, as Jewish, has enclaves in Palestine. As a result, this kind of recognition endangers the national identity of the Palestinian state since it allows its Jewish inhabitants to be citizens of another country, of Israel.

To understand their dilemma, one need only listen to the Israeli consensual discourse that defines the return of Palestinian refugees, even in small numbers, as a red line that should not be crossed. Any added Palestinian to Israel is perceived as a menace to its Jewish identity. The Palestinians' other choice is to redefine their territorial identity, and squeeze their national dreams into the borders which will be defined by the settlers.

The Palestinians, needless to say, do not want Jewish settlers inside their future state as much as Israel does not want their refugees. It is not about real estate and square kilometers, as much as it is about the mutual fear of losing the national identity. Palestine, so say the settlers, cannot be Judenrein; likewise, Palestinians may argue that Israel cannot be Palestinianrein.[12]

The result is that Israel and the Palestinians are locked in internal negotiations with their enclaves and not with each other. These internal negotiations demonstrated their futility when the US administration succeeded in pressuring Israel into adopting the freeze on building in the West Bank for ten months. It was a test case to check not just how serious the Israeli government was in claiming that it was ready to implement confidence-building measures, but rather if it was capable of dealing with the settlers. For the first time, Israel's sovereignty was put to the test, and the state had to demonstrate whether it was occupying the settlers or being occupied by them.

A freezing process

Although the planned freeze was only partly applied, it became an important symbol, but altogether it was a mistake. The US administration should have told Israel from the outset: do not freeze settlement construction, do not stop it in part or for a period, not for six months, not for a single day. As long as the US administration does not present a comprehensive plan that explains its endgame—what the end will look like and what the shape and character of the Palestinian state will look like—the demand for a cessation of construction is pointless. It is a pathetic return to the doctrine of confidence-building measures, which led nowhere. The demand to freeze settlements' construction is similar to the demand to remove roadblocks or cease razing homes; all these demands meant only one thing: making the continuation of the occupation a little more pleasant.

The demand for a cessation of settlements' construction will have no impact on the political process as long as the United States and its partners in the Quartet are not telling the Israeli and Palestinian publics what will happen with the Israelis who already live in the West Bank and East Jerusalem. How many of them will have to be evacuated? How much money will this cost and who will pay for it? The evacuation of 7,000 Jews from the Gaza Strip cost more than NIS 10 billion.[13] Even if only 100,000 Jews are to be evacuated from the West Bank, based on this estimate, the move will cost some NIS 150 billion—about 50 percent of the national budget for an entire year. It is true that it amounts to *only* about 8 percent of the cost of the American war in Iraq to date, and maybe for the sake of peace in the Middle East the US administration would be willing to invest another 8 percent in the area, but someone in Washington must articulate this clearly. That would be much more convincing than halting the work of a crane.

The US pressure yielded an impressive achievement when it twisted Prime Minister Benjamin Netanyahu's arm and got him to say that he wants "two states for two peoples." Nevertheless, what comes next? Are Netanyahu's two states the same as the Palestinians' vision of two states? Moreover, are they the same two states as Washington envisions? Where will the borderline be between the two states? After all, if it is agreed that, by the end of the process, some settlements' blocs will remain in Israel's hands, and if indeed the Palestinians accept this in return for an exchange of territory, why is it necessary to cease construction in those blocs? Logic dictates that construction should continue in the blocs and at a faster pace, so that it will be possible to absorb those evacuated settlers from other settlements. However, when there is no plan or agreement on the border, not to mention that negotiations are not even taking place, the demand for ceasing construction appears to be some sort of an independent aim, isolated from any political context, whose sole intention is to display the US's ability to impose "something" on Israel.

The attempt to understand the US policy as a tactical action that intends to lead to further actions is heading toward a dead end and might even be dangerous. Because it is not the public in Israel that needs to be encouraged; it is the right-wing government, for whom the remnants of the Labor Party are serving as apologists, that needs to be persuaded. Worse yet, this government may agree to a gradual and temporary cessation of settlements' construction, while at the same time it will make every effort to prove that there is no partner that is worth this "sacrifice" on the other side. At the end of the settlements' construction freeze, the government will be able to celebrate the failure of the negotiations and to prove to Washington that the pressure has been put on the wrong side. The chance of restarting the process from there will be nil.

An honest government would not have to rely on an Arab safety net in order to restart the process. It would have taken advantage of the long period of calm in the West Bank and Gaza Strip; the efficiency that the Palestinian security forces have demonstrated in the West Bank in combating terrorism, and the willingness of Abbas to negotiate seriously, in order to tell the public that the quota of confidence-building measures has been fulfilled, and that the time has come for withdrawing from the occupied territories and reaching an agreement.

However, this is not the kind of government that is running Israel. Washington knows this, as every Israeli citizen does. Hence, the need for a comprehensive plan that will be managed with precision, determination, and international supervision. Freezing the settlements is not a plan nor is it a prescription for peace. It freezes the process while empowering the settlers' control over Israel's foreign policy.

The world is watching

While the freeze on construction in the settlements has become a touchstone for Israel's intentions and its ability to negotiate with its inner opposition, namely, the settlers, a more "menacing" threat is looming at the horizons. The intended call for an international recognition of an independent Palestinian state at the UN is perceived in Israel as the ultimate blow to its strategy.

It is not within the scope of this chapter to analyze the legal and security aspects and implications on Israel and the Palestinians once a Palestinian state is declared. However, it is important to understand how the internal debate between the Israeli government and the settlers, on the one hand, and between the Palestinian authority and Hamas, on the other hand, can influence the international political map toward the conflict and the parties involved.

The parallelograms of forces inside Israel and the occupied territories demonstrate clearly that the Israeli government's position is the exact opposite of that of the Palestinian authority. However, what about Hamas and the settlers? Here, we may find an unsurprising common denominator. The settlers and Hamas are against a Palestinian state, at least in the shape and form that are suggested by Mahmud Abbas.[14] Paradoxically, the United States finds itself in the same trench with Israel, Hamas, and the settlers. The difference between these three parties is that, while Hamas and the settlers have the power of veto over their respective governments' decisions, but not at the international arena, the United States can veto any international decision concerning a Palestinian state, but it does not have any veto power in the internal Palestinian or Israeli spheres. This construction will remain stable as long as the settlers are able to rely on the Israeli government to adhere to their positions. For that to happen, the settlers will need to maintain enough leverage in order to convince the government that not only its political future is at risk, but also the future or at least the security of Israel is at risk if a Palestinian state is to be established.

The settlers' problem is that into the familiar parallelogram of forces—one that they know how to manipulate—new components are involved. These are the 135-odd states that have already expressed their support for a Palestinian state, and, not less important, the new pro-democracy revolutions that have taken place in Middle East. These new elements may put the US administration at odds with its own declared policy. Will it be able to resist the will of an overwhelming majority of UN members, some of which are strong allies of the US? Will Obama be able to reconcile his objection to a unilaterally declared independent Palestinian state with his support for the new revolutionaries in the Middle East who strive to create new democratic regimes? How will the US be able to establish good relations with Arab publics while refusing to grant its support to its own policy of "two states for two peoples"?

These dilemmas place the settlers and Hamas in a new context. From local powers that can dictate policies to their *homeland-states*, they become players in the international stage. This is where another paradox is evolving. If the US intends to adhere to its opposition to the Palestinians' initiative at the UN, it needs Hamas to adhere to its traditional policy, and, if it wants serious negotiations between Israel and the Palestinians, it has to come to terms with the settlers. Hence, once again, non-governmental organizations may influence not only the status of the Israeli and Palestinian future but also the US status in the world or at least in the Middle East.

Yet, if the political conflict endangers the US status in the Middle East as General David Petraeus alluded to, the struggle over the identity of the State of Israel will and must engage Diaspora Jews in general and American Jews in particular.[15] As the settlers enjoy a temporary lull in their struggle against the peace process, they and their partners in the Knesset have found the time to promote their ideological agenda. This time they have embarked on confronting the attempts to boycott products that are manufactured in the settlements. On 11 July 2011, a majority of 47 against 38 Members of Knesset approved what is tagged as the "boycott law."[16] Apart from its draconian stipulations and its apparent contradictions to freedom of speech as defined in the Israeli law, it demonstrates the extent of influence that the settlements have on the character of the State of Israel. In essence, this law, which aims at protecting the settlements' economic well-being, implies, above all, that the settlements are not just part and parcel of Israel, but that the Motherland is willing to bend its values for the sake of the settlers. In other words, whoever intends to harm the settlements, inside Israel or abroad, the state will reach him. This step goes far beyond justified military protection of the settlers and the settlements by the state. This law puts the state not just at the service of the settlements; it also declares that the Israeli values are hostage to the settlements' policy and practice. In fact, it clarifies that the future identity of Israel will be outlined by an inner-Diaspora that considers the state a tool to promote its ideology.

This trend should be worrisome not just to Israeli citizens—it should worry every Jew who sees in the State of Israel the embodiment of Jewish liberal values.

Can there be a solution?

It is just too easy to dismiss the question with a flat "no." Israel and the Palestinians have made a long way together; they know each other more than any rival people do, they understand that a one-state solution will be disastrous for both, and they realize that a four-states situation is untenable. These are enough points of departure for a reasonable solution. However, there are six conditions to be fulfilled for these points to become a serious launch pad for a political solution.

A   Israel has to consider the settlements as debatable, thus, negotiable territory.
B   Israel has to adopt the idea that the settlers derive their identity from Israel, and not vice versa.
C   The Palestinians have to recognize Israel's limits of power in dealing with the settlements, and adopt a more realistic approach toward land sharing. On the other hand, Israel should be more generous in offering a higher percentage of land to be exchanged. After all, if settlements are so important, they should not be valued only by the dimension of their geographic space.
D   Israel has to recognize that there is one Palestinian people, not two. If there is a rift between Fatah and Hamas, it is not for Israel to manipulate it. Hence, Israel does not need to recognize Hamas or a separate state in Gaza; it should recognize the Palestinian government even if Hamas is part of it.
E   The United States has to become an active partner in the negotiations, not merely a facilitator or a navigator. It has to consider solving the conflict as part of its national interest and not just that of the "parties involved."
F   Diaspora Jews cannot stay aloof in the face of the identity change that is developing in Israel. They should understand that one cannot stay liberal abroad, while identifying with a non-liberal, occupying regime.

These conditions are not easy to accomplish, but they are based on some new premises that may appeal to both sides as they address two basic principles that have hindered any advance in the peace process so far.

First, it will abolish the situation where the settlements and settlers are designing Israel's policy. Second, the principle of "Land for Peace" will be defined by value and not by volume.

This approach is worth trying, yet it demands a different type of leadership on both sides. We can get there, but we have a little problem with time limits.

The Israeli and the Palestinian generations who still remember what it was like to be friends are fading away, and the new generations will have to imagine peace; they will need a vision, but vision is what we lack right now.

In the meantime, and while the Middle East is embroiled in revolutionary and violent attempts to fulfill democratic visions, Israel seems to be immune to international pressure to produce a plan for solving its conflict with the Palestinians.

However, in this time gap, Israel is pushing ahead to crystallize its identity as a Jewish state. An identity that draws its pattern not from liberalism but from dictates which were imposed on it by the *inner-Diaspora*, the settlers, who in the course of 40 years made Israel their satellite state.

Notes

1 Donnan Hastings and Thomas M. Wilson, *Borders: Frontiers of Identity, Nation and State*, Oxford: Berg, 2001, p. 4.
2 Ulrich Beck, *What Is Globalization?* Malden, UK: Blackwell, 2000; Eric Hobsbawm, *Nations and Nationalism Since 1780: Programme, Myth, Reality*, Cambridge: Cambridge University Press, 1991; Benedict Anderson, *Imagined Communities*, London: Verso, 1983; Clifford Geertz, *The Interpretation of Cultures: Selected Essays*, New York: Basic, 1973.
3 See Amnon Rubinstein, *From Herzl to Gush Emunim and Back* [in Hebrew], Tel Aviv: Schoken, 1980, pp. 89–93.
4 For further discussion, see Moshe Dayan, *On the Peace Process and the Future of Israel* [in Hebrew], Tel Aviv: Ministry of Defense, 1988.
5 See Menachem Hofnung, *Israel: Security Needs Vs the Rule of Law*, Jerusalem: Nevo, 1991; Baruch Kimmerling, *The Interrupted System: Israel Civilians in War and Routine Times*, New Brunswick and London: Transaction Books, 1985; Gershon Kieval, *Party Politics in Israel and the Occupied Territories*, Westport: Greenwood, 1983.
6 For detailed discussion about the settlements' status as military outposts, see Moshe Negbi, *Justice Under Occupation*, Jerusalem: Kana, 1981.
7 See Hofnung, *Israel: Security Needs Vs the Rule of Law*; Moshe Negbi, *Above the Law: The Constitutional Crisis in Israel*, Tel Aviv: Am Oved, 1987; Rubinstein, "The Changing Status of the Territories," in *I'yunei Mishpat*, Smadar Otolengi (ed.), Tel Aviv: Tel Aviv University Press, 1986, pp. 439—56; Moshe Drori, "Israeli Settlement in Judea and Samaria: Legal Aspects," in *Ir Ve'ezor* [City and Region], vol. 4, no. 3, 1981, 28: 45.
8 Hofnung, *Israel: Security Needs Vs the Rule of Law*, pp. 293–397.
9 One example is Prof. Zeev Sternhell's article in *Haaretz*, "Against a Lunatic Government," 5 May 2001 [in Hebrew], which created an uproar among settlers and right-wing politicians in Israel. Sternhell was accused of "promoting killing of settlers" by Palestinians. Available at <http://www.haaretz.co.il/misc/1.700439>.
10 For further discussion on the settlers' campaign to mobilize non-religious publics, see Rubinstein, *From Herzl to Gush Emunim and Back*.
11 In numerous interviews, Abbas adheres to the unity of the Palestinian states as it was agreed also by Israel in the Oslo Agreements.
12 For an example of the Israeli right-wing position, see Moshe Arens, "Judenrein Palestine," *Haaretz*, 4 August 2008. Available at <www.haaretz.com/print-edition/opinion/judenrein-palestine-1.243549>.
13 For a comprehensive analysis of the economic implications of the disengagement plan from Gaza, see David Brodet (ed.), "The Cost of Disengagement: Economic

Implications" [in Hebrew], *Policy Research,* 64, July 2005, Israel Democracy Institute. Available at <http://www.idi.org.il/PublicationsCatalog/Pages/PP_64/Publications_Catalog_2064.aspx>.

14 According to cables which were exposed by WikiLeaks, even moderate leaders among the settlers do not see it as an option to accept a Palestinian state. See <www.haaretz.co.il/hasite/spages/1224123.html>. For Hamas' position, see Khaled Mashaal's quotation where he does not oppose a Palestinian state but puts forward the right of return for the refugees and not "giving up even one span of the hand of our land" as preconditions. See <http://arabic.ruvr.ru/2011/05/04/49841247.html>.

15 See "Statement of General David H. Petraeus, U.S. Army Commander, U.S. Central Command before the Senate Armed Services Committee on the Posture of U.S. Central Command," 16 March 2010. Available at <http://armed-services.senate.gov/statemnt/2010/03%20March/Petraeus%2003-16-10.pdf>.

16 For the full text of the law in Hebrew, see <http://www.acri.org.il/he/wp-content/uploads/2011/07/boycottlaw.pdf>. For an unofficial translation to English, see "Bill for Prevention of Damage to the State of Israel through Boycott, 2011," British Committee for the Universities of Palestine. Available at <http://www.bricup.org.uk/news/BoycottLaw2011text.html>.

8   Judaism and Islam in the World

Rabbi Michael Melchior

Since the earliest recorded history of humankind, religion, in its ideal form, has been the major source of life, future, and redemption. At the same time, it has been abused as the ultimate source of fear, hatred, strife, war, and death. The Talmud paraphrased this accurately by equating the holy Torah to the tree of life, which, when misused, becomes the drug of death.[1]

The first chronicled killing in the Bible is the murder of Abel by his brother Cain.[2] It is obvious from the biblical story that this murder is closely entwined with religion. Perhaps the murder takes place against the backdrop of a sibling rivalry over whose sacrifice is accepted by God, as the Scriptures tell us. Or perhaps it is the outcome of a violent argument between them, concerning whose land the Temple should be built on, according to rabbinical commentary.[3] In either case, religion, in the primary narrative of the human condition, is the cause of envy and strife. The idea that the physical location of the Temple, the place where humans connect with their Creator, could be shared, already at this early stage of the narrative, did not seem to occur to the protagonists, even though there were very few people around, and those who were around were brothers. The totalitarianism of religion had already taken a dominant place, a place that was to remain permanent and central throughout human history.

Religion has been a major factor, if not the major factor, in both international relations and domestic politics around the world; very often, it is found at the core of wars and conflict. While this has been the case throughout human history, this was, to a certain degree, less true in the twentieth century. From the outset of the First World War until the fall of the Berlin Wall, the source of major wars and genocides cannot primarily be traced back to religion. However, already from the beginning of the twenty-first century, it can be said that God has returned to the forefront of history, as religion has reemerged as a dominant factor all over the world.

Again, religion plays a dual role. On the one hand, religion enriches human existence by committing one to fundamental values regarding the human condition and survival. Yet, on the other hand, religion serves as a dramatic source of conflict in nearly all of the 20-odd major conflicts and wars currently raging in different regions of the world. Whether in Sri Lanka, Kashmir,

Nigeria, Iraq, Cyprus, or our part of the Middle East, religion is at the focal point of today's bloody conflicts.

While there can be no peace among nations until there is peace among religions, to quote Professor Hans Kung,[4] those involved in these conflicts as well as those who are assisting in trying to resolve the conflicts, choose to ignore this truth. The reasons for this purposeful ignorance are manifold. Perhaps it is much easier ignoring this truth than dealing with it; or maybe it is because religion was hardly ever dealt with in the context of conflict resolution; or it might be due to a generally accepted convention among politicians, academics, and opinion-makers that nothing peaceful could ever emanate from religion. This is an axiom that I, as a staunch believer in religion, can never accept. At the same time, I also cannot deny that there seems to be some truth to the aforementioned concept when I look at the world and see how religion is used and abused by religious and political leaders alike.

The problem with this approach is that disregarding the religious elements of conflicts does not lead to their resolution. Rather, these issues fester and grow, making conflicts more intractable, shattering our hopes of building a more just and peaceful future. More problematic still is that even in classical national conflicts—which generally are not rooted in religion, but contain religious and cultural elements—the more totalitarian forces of religion have been able to step up and dominate, filling a vacuum created by the disregard of these very elements. As such, these secular national conflicts have turned into clashes between religions and civilizations.

Since the outset of the Middle East conflict, the clash between religions has been a major component. Even the socialist-atheist-Zionist fathers could paraphrase their relationship to God and the land by saying that "while we do not believe in the existence of a God, He certainly did promise us the land." Since the beginning, the conflict has also had very deep religious roots for the Arabs. The appeal to religious legitimacy from both sides was very dominant, both before the creation of the State of Israel and, in many ways, during the War of Independence. This appeal to religion is still relevant today: the vast majority of people in Israel,[5] the Palestinian area, and the Middle East at large are religious, or at least look toward religion and tradition as a major source of personal and communal identity and legitimization. Because the peace process is seen as a threat to this religion-based identity, the processes and the leaders involved become an existential threat in their opponents' eyes.

Regardless, it has become evident that the secular peace has little cred- ibility, not only in theological terms, but also in the sense that such a peace is not sustainable and does not have the potential to create the kind of future that its promoters promise. No matter how good Shimon Peres' intentions were when he introduced the concept of the *New Middle East*, in the minds of the believers, this is a Middle East which promotes the cheapest brand of Western values, while, on its path, it crushes traditional ethics and patterns of familial and community living. With the language of mistrust, fear, and distorted perceptions prevailing on both sides, nothing is easier than to play the religious card and, in doing so, turn fear into hatred and violence, tragically eliminating hope and belief that peace is actually possible.

Until recently, even the serious peacemakers had decided to strategically ignore the religious element. In my own personal outcry against this attempt, which I have been promoting with the same persistence as the claim of Cato the Elder for the last 25 years, I have not even aroused sufficient interest to be dismissed. Yossi Beilin, probably the most courageous and innovative of the peacemakers on the Israeli side, is one of the few who has been able to relate to my argument at all. However, even since before the Oslo Accords, he has been telling me that, while in theory I might be right, he and his colleagues would lead a "quick fix" peace deal, and that only in its aftermath—just as with the Truth and Reconciliation Commission in South Africa—will we approach and try to solve the underlying existential issues, which no doubt need to be dealt with. I supported this approach, always wanting to give peace a chance. In trying to prove myself wrong, I did not believe in putting preconditions on any process. On a certain level, I still advocate this approach. I fully supported the Oslo Accords, even though I was skeptical about the possibility of its success, precisely because of the exclusion of the religious element. However, I felt that the historic attempt to create a new relationship with the Palestinian nation was in itself a kind of religious act, although that was certainly not the intention. We humans are supposed to emulate the ways of God, "Imitato Dei," just as He makes peace in the heavens;[6] it is the first imperative that we do our utmost to make peace and eliminate bloodshed on earth.

During the 1990s, I participated in a variety of people-to-people efforts, peace initiatives, and negotiations all over the world. I went into politics, and served as a cabinet minister in the Barak government. I even had a minor part in the unfortunate Camp David negotiations that took place in the summer of 2000. As an anecdote of that period, I built, together with Jewish, Christian, and Muslim leaders, a concept of religious peace in Jerusalem and a model for a viable solution for the issues concerning the Old City. I approached Barak before Camp David, offering him these ideas on a silver platter. He totally dismissed them, assuring me that he would succeed in reaching an agreement and that involving religious leaders and religious issues would only mess things up.

What really messed things up was the way in which this issue was dealt with at Camp David. In a completely misconceived desire to appease the Jewish religious opposition to a compromise on the Jerusalem issue, Barak suggested building a synagogue on the Temple Mount. This suggestion reinforced Arafat's negation of any Jewish connection and aspiration to the Temple Mount, while President Clinton, having just returned from church, listening there to the words of Jesus preaching to his disciples in the Temple, did not understand how this could be. How could Jesus have preached in a place that according to Arafat never existed, or, at the very least, was never a Jewish Temple?

Clinton then came up with a very innovative but hopeless proposal that the Temple Mount be divided horizontally, with Israeli sovereignty under the ground, and Palestinian above ground. This concept, which Clinton no doubt received from the Israeli team, fed into Barak's misconception of what he called "Kodshei Yisrael" (the Holies of Israel), which he understood to be archaeological relics from the Temple. This idea again fed into the false Muslim narrative that Jews have no real connection to this holy place, and that we just want underground control in order to blow up the Muslim holy sites. Thus, while Barak claimed that proactively dealing with the issue of religion would only hinder efforts to reach an agreement, he inadvertently helped set in motion a process that inculcated the religious element into every aspect of the conflict. Ultimately, the second *intifada*, which began in 2000, was dubbed by the Palestinians the "Al-Aqsa Intifada," named after the mosque on the Temple Mount. The religious sentiment had turned very much into the core issue.

As a result of my active political involvement, over the next decade I became convinced that ignoring or postponing the dealings with the religious existential components of the conflict had not made, and would never make them disappear. Rather, skirting around these issues turned them into the main obstacle to the success of any attempt at peace, even in the few cases when these attempts were sincere. Time and again, the religious delegitimization of the peace process has set us back, preventing these attempts from leading us forward.

On the Islamic side, this is evident with the growth of radical Islam. The world Jihad established branches amongst the Palestinians as did the Muslim Brotherhood. Its branch, Hamas very rapidly developed from an educational, social, cultural, and religious institution into a leading radical totalitarian political force. Hamas had the spiritual, political, and physical will and power to disrupt the process. The success of Hamas and its ability to deliver does not only stem from the failures and corruption of Fatah, but also from its constituting a serious political and religious force which, as most people have now come to realize, just cannot be ignored.

Also on the Jewish side, although in a different way, religion and even the name of God Himself have been hijacked and distorted in order to delegitimize the political peace process. After Oslo, Baruch Goldstein and Yigal Amir became extreme catastrophic expressions of this ever-growing delegitimization. The political objection to uprooting settlements or even freezing their construction is rooted in a religious messianic expression of our future, which makes it impossible to proceed politically. The formal religious-legal argument laid down is the strict prohibition to give up land, no matter what the price. Yet, from a religious-legal perspective, this could easily be solved because the vast majority of Halachic authorities would agree that it is permitted to give up land for peace. The issues involved here, however, reach far beyond the legal aspects and into the ideological, messianic vision of this branch of religious Zionism. According to this vision, we are so close to the messianic condition that we do not need to consider the world of "real-politik." God will provide as He did in the War of Independence, in the "liberation" of Jerusalem and Judea and Samaria in the Six-Day War, and also in hardening the hearts of Israel's enemies, not letting them agree to compromise.

The ultra-orthodox element, which for various reasons was indifferent or neutral to the peace process in the early stages, has become still more nationalistic and hateful toward the other side of the conflict. Furthermore, because some of the elements among the peacemakers have seen peace in the context of the ultimate secularization of our societies, the orthodox constituents are currently utilizing their growing political power to halt any real progress in the peace process. This is the real reason why we need to look not only at what the peace process contains, but also at what it lacks. The peace process does *not* need yet another summit meeting in Washington, Paris, or Sharm el-Sheikh; it does *not* need yet another road map, or a suggestion for a political deal. That deal has been known to all parties, at least since the Clinton proposals in 2000. How many blind alleys do we need to go down before we halt and ask ourselves why it's not working?

What *is* needed today, for both Jews and Arabs alike, is a restored belief and trust that there is indeed a partner on the other side; a partner who has the legitimacy and support to be able to create and sign a comprehensive peace agreement, which will actually be implemented and will transform our future.

Today, nearly all of those involved in peace efforts would agree that, if the process were to harness the power of the mainstream religious identities and legitimization, this would create the energy and confidence needed to shift the current paradigm and end the dangerous present stalemate. I stress that this should be done not as a substitute for the political process and its leaders, but as a complement to them. The unification of the religious and political components of the process will empower and give credibility to the involved leaders' wishes to create a new reality for our peoples.

This fusion of the political and the religious also applies to the opportunities that have presented themselves as a result of the events of the "Arab Spring." Instead of just looking at the dangers taking shape in the new Arab world, I believe that we must also look at the immense potential presented by the current regional situation, primarily as it relates to basic Jewish ethics. I believe we should be pleased when nations rise up against regimes of torture, despotism and slavery. However, prior to any political consideration, I believe that as Jews we should be moved by the magnitude of the changes taking place in the Arab world from the point of view of Jewish ethics, emanating from the belief in a Torah which confirms and validates every human being's basic rights, the freedom of man, and the Divine dignity of every human being.

While it is true that, on the political plain, there was a great blessing in the peace agreement with Egypt, we must not forget that this was a peace agreement contracted with an autocratic dictator. This was not a genuine peace based on common values that would have led to the creation of an honest and open relationship with the Egyptian people. Moreover, as is true of many tyrants, the Egyptian despot used anti-Semitism as a shock absorber in order to divert the opposition's criticism leveled at him toward the Jewish people and the State of Israel.

I saw this with my own eyes in 2002, when my Palestinian counterpart, the late Sheikh Talal Sider, and I convened a summit meeting in Alexandria, Egypt, which included all of the major religious leaders of the three mono-theistic religions for the first time in history. We organized the meeting under the auspices of the late Grand Imam of al-Azhar Mosque and Grand Sheikh of al-Azhar University, Muhammad Sayyid Tantawi; the Archbishop of Canterbury, Lord George Carey; and Israel's Chief Rabbi, Rabbi Eliyahu Bakshi-Doron. The summit, which launched The Alexandria Process, brought together religious leaders from the Middle East to adopt common principles aimed at preventing the region's religious sensibilities from being exploited during conflicts, and declaring the need to work together toward peaceful solutions to interreligious conflicts.

In proximity to this meeting, some of us sat with Egyptian President Hosni Mubarak. At this encounter, I expressed my concern to him regarding the anti-Semitism that flourished in the state media of his country. I told Mubarak that I believe that no peace can ever be built when accompanied with stereotypical lies about the other. Mubarak responded with a statement that revealed his tactics: "You don't understand," he said, "those who oppose me the most are also the worst anti-Semites." What he wanted to say was that this is how they find some release for their expressions of hostility and hatred. They have two options: to hate us or to hate him. And for some reason he preferred the former.

Consequently, an immense barrier has formed between Jews and Israelis on one side and the Egyptian people on the other, in spite of the formal peace. There is no doubt, however, for those who are following the changes in Egypt and most of the Arab world, that the vast majority of the people there are religious. However, this does not mean that they all become part of the most extreme totalitarian expressions of religion, or that they throw themselves into the arms and the advocacy of Ahmadinejad or al-Qaeda. Rather, this fact definitely says something very important about the place of religion in building the future and the new identity of this region. The widespread reli-giosity of people living in this region also opens windows of opportunity that we have never seen before. If we could solve our conflict with the Palestinians on the basis of a genuine peace between our religions based on a religious and legal legitimization of the two-state solution, then we would have a real opportu-nity to connect with each other in this area which we both inhabit, and make peace with the rest of the Arab and Muslim worlds.

Now, while most could agree with this theory, they would also claim that it is simply not possible. This pessimistic approach would merely strengthen the common conviction of the infeasibility of peace in this area. As such, we would need to be reconciled to this reality, try to control the situation as best as we can, and live for the foreseeable future by the strength of our swords. This despair will once again expand the vacuum into which the extremists and enemies on both sides can play their trump cards.

For a long time now, it has been beyond me how governments and inter-national non-governmental organizations believe that they can seriously promote peace through people-to-people initiatives that served only to "preach to the converted." These programs reached out to people from the left-wing fringe, who lack the legitimacy and power to move anybody but themselves. Hundreds of millions of dollars have been poured into these efforts with little results to show. Interreligious events have been organized in the same style: official leaders, in their photogenic hats and gowns, came together to declare that their religions are synonymous with peace. Saying this, they turned around and went home, where they continue to preach that such a messianic peace can obviously be obtained only through the elimination of the other side, at least spiritually.

For several years, I have tried to identify and develop a different approach. This has led me to work head-on with mainstream Imams and teachers from the Islamic Movement, who have great influence in their communities and societies. They are not numbered among the peacemakers, but rather are skeptical, even in total opposition to the political peace processes. Therefore, both my Jewish and Islamic colleagues have had to invent a new discipline—a systematic approach to conflict resolution in the religious existential context. This is something that hardly exists anywhere in the world. During this process, I have been able to secretly participate in Islamic summit meetings even in countries with which Israel has no diplomatic relations, speaking as an orthodox rabbi, a devoted Zionist, and, at times, as an Israeli official—all the while traveling on an Israeli passport.

Through these experiences, I have learned a lot, from both my own mistakes and those of others. However, the good news is that I have always returned optimistic, having seen that, even at the worst and most difficult levels, it is possible to make the walls of hatred and suspicion come tumbling down.

In order to succeed, this new religious approach will need to be totally different than the secular political approach, which is the accepted wisdom in the modern Western world. Although there are various models of separation between Church and state in the Western world, conceptually there is a clear divide. What belongs to the Church is up to the personal belief of the individual and has no place in the public domain of decision-making—not within the state, and certainly not in the context of relations between states. Secularization theorists limit the scope of religion to the area of ritual; at most, they expand it to the realm of family-legislation, and rules of modesty and inter-human relationships. This confines religion safely inside the realm of Church and home, minimizing the contribution of religion to issues of the public sphere at large, such as economy, society, justice, relation to the "other," environment, foreign policies, war, and peace.

When the Western world deals with the rest of the world, it naturally holds its own culture, values, and ideas, and reads the rest of the world through the eyes of these parameters. I believe that this inability to understand the world around us often has tragic consequences. Former American Secretary of State Dr. Madeleine Albright presents a very important analysis of the consequences of this Western approach in her book *The Mighty and The Almighty*.[7]

Unfortunately, I see clear repetition of the same pattern of mistakes in the media commentary on and political dealings with the Islamic parties, which have risen to power through elections in the aftermath of the so-called Arab Spring. These are parties and ideological movements that have evolved under circumstances of the persecuted opposition for many years; they have had no political power and very little influence and responsibility.

In line with the thinking and dialogue that I have been able to develop over recent years, together with my Jewish and Muslim colleagues, I would like to suggest an alternative to the conventional Western wisdom. Put aside the approach of segregating Church and state. Put aside the concept of dichotomous thinking which tells the Islamic parties like the Islamic Brotherhood in Egypt that they can have their measure of religion but need to, for the sake of managing their country and dealing with the real world, keep up a certain element of democracy, women's rights, relationships with the non-Muslim world, and respect for signed treaties (e.g., peace with Israel, etc.) as a pragmatic measure in order to be able to continue to receive US military and civil support and income from tourism, in order to be able to feed an ever-growing population.

The Western approach might work for a very short period, but it will collapse because it has no base in the truth of tradition or any fundamental values. My suggestion bases itself on a dialectic approach, which accepts that, for a religious person, everything comes from God and all values exist within the religious system. The dialectic approach acknowledges, of course, that there constantly exists a clash of values and that a responsible religious leader often needs to make very difficult decisions in order to serve God. This really means to serve his community and his society in the best way possible as a truly religious decision within the framework of religious law, not because he is pressured from outside, but because this is what it means to be an obedient servant of God.

In Judaism, this is certainly the basis for all normative Jewish thinking. When the holy Temple was destroyed 2,000 years ago, and the Jewish people lost its national, religious, and judicial center, it was dispersed to all corners of the earth. The substitute to this center became the dichotomous study of the oral law and tradition. Jews held onto very few dogmas and fundamentals, while they held onto many essential ideas and values, which, in different situations of life, clashed with each other and had to be debated and resolved, again and again, in order to address the human condition and search for legal and ethical priorities and answers to difficult dilemmas in life. This tradition of learning and thinking travelled and developed with the Jew whenever and wherever he lived. This made it possible for the Jew to deal with different living situations and values. This made it possible for him to think outside of the box, something very often misunderstood and/or unappreciated by our neighbors, but necessary for both the physical and spiritual survival of the Jewish people. Although not identical, parallel traditions exist in Christianity and very much so in the Islamic traditions. There exists in the dichotomous process of interpretation of the sharia law a hierarchy of values, which are translated into religious decisions and interpretations every day.

I have witnessed in my dealings and debates with the Islamists, courageous visionary leaders grappling with the fundamental issues of religion and modernity, Islamic law and democracy, not only as a basis for getting elected and misusing ones majority in order to dominate society, but also in the context of the basic issues of freedom of speech, freedom of and from religion, and minority rights, both individual and collective. These deliberations do not stem from pressure from Western governments or intellectuals but from a continuous line of Islamic thinking and as a result of fatwas written over generations, and this thinking is affected by the way Islam looks at humanity at large today. It might see that humanity has made considerable progress when it comes to certain aspects of human rights and dignity when compared to the situation throughout history, when many of the important legal writings of Islam were compiled. On the other hand, the world today may be a less protected place when it comes to the observance of traditional values such as decency, family, the respect for fellow human beings, etc.

Among these crucial concerns, the matters of creating a religious peace between the monotheistic religions and giving religious motivation and authorization to the peace process and the two-state solution have also emerged. On the Jewish side, I have been able to identify religious mainstream leaders who nobody would believe could be a part of this process, including some Shas and settler rabbis as well as their supporters, who have also put forward innovative solutions for some of the very difficult political issues on the table.

The burden of proof is totally on us. Therefore, the main challenge that we face is how to take responsibility for an authentic religious process, which can transform religion from being a destructive and deadly sword, into being a powerful lever for pursuing and obtaining peace. Is it really possible to change the role of religion, from the core of the problem into the source of its solution?

The latest developments in the Arab world might help us in creating a synthesis between a deep commitment to religious, traditional, ethical, and moral values, together with an equally deep commitment to peace. Many of us, for too long, have isolated ourselves on our little clouds, with our totalitarian truths, not relating to events on the ground or truly taking responsibility for the physical and spiritual well-being of our believers and societies. This period must end.

Now is the time for the real test. I believe that interreligious peace dialogue could become the ladder with which we can make our way back down to earth, reconnect with what is happening on the ground and take responsibility, without losing any contact with heaven above. This ladder is firmly rooted in the belief in one God and His word, the modesty of man, knowing the limitation of human understanding and power, and a conviction that we are here on this earth not to replace, but to serve God. God cannot be honored by crushing His creations and creatures. This ladder must be deeply embedded in ethical values common to the believers in one God, freedom, justice, peace, morality, and ethics.

While knowing who we are, and understanding the boundaries between our beliefs, we can find a common fertile ground on which a very different Middle East can grow. We need to introduce a religious language that has been excluded from the process until now. In this language, land is not real estate that you can annex or get rid of as seen opportune at any given moment. In this language, you should not give up your ultimate dreams and quests, which are legitimate, but you can support giving up land for true peace, if this can promote other religious values such as the good of your community, the sanctity of human life, and spreading the respect for religion and religious commitment. In the dialectic thinking of a clash of values, this is even simpler. Instead of a fair secular debate in Israel, the Israeli left won the debate by promoting a peace driven by fear of "the other" and therefore lost in terms of morality. The left led the public to believe that we need to divide the country because we fear the demographic growth of the Arabs; that they will outnumber us. But you cannot build true peace if your main phobia is the womb of the Arab woman. This only leads to the far more dangerous approaches of separation or apartheid promoted by Lieberman and Kahane.

Our approach is different. Out of a common belief in the same God, who demands of all of His believers in the Holy Land to prefer life over land, let us use our senses of morality and justice to build two states, living in peace with each other, with open borders, with a large Arab Palestinian minority living in the State of Israel, and a Jewish minority living also in the State of Palestine. Both traditions have an element of sanctity of the land, but this tradition must always be put aside when it conflicts with the values of the sanctity and dignity of human life. However, this does not mean that we need to give up our ultimate dreams.

The Talmud talks about a decision of a religious court: two people appear in front of the court holding onto two ends of the same cloth, each claiming it to be their own. The Talmud says that they both have to swear that at least half is theirs, and then they have to divide it into two.[8] By only swearing that half is theirs, the court, in a sophisticated manner, prevents one of the parties from becoming a perjurer, which would otherwise happen if both would have to swear that it was all theirs. At the same time, the court does not exclude either claim to or quest for the totality. This is a religious legalistic approach, which has deep roots in both Jewish and Islamic thinking; both accommodate for pragmatism, without losing sight of the overall vision. Having reached this common ground, we might be able to lift ourselves up to the next level and recognize that eventually the land, all of the land, belongs to God the Almighty, and that we are here on earth as temporary residents. Observing this aspect of human existence, we can then view issues of territory and sovereignty with a very different perception. No believer can dismiss this concept. Although it might be perceived as naïve in the political context, the naïveté itself is a religious ideal.

This message will have a dramatic effect all over the world that, if we can—and we can—work it out in Jerusalem, there is no reason not to do so in Baghdad, Kaduna, Derry, or the slums of Paris. The dramatic effect that this will create inside Israel and for Israel's relations with the world will be transformative. For too long, our actions and reactions have been built on and led by our fears. These fears have not been unfounded; not for one day have we had peace; not for one day has there not been someone in our vicinity calling to wipe us out. Not for one day have we even known where our borders are.

Aside from the unnecessary urge to constantly defend ourselves, our fears have led to many destructive results on which it is impossible to build a sane future. The fear has developed phobias inside our society and has built a growing abyss between us and the parts of the world with which we could and should cooperate. The message of religious peace and its consequences for our relations with our neighbors will place us in the role to repair our world by building a new world together with our neighbors—a role which, for many Jews, is the essence of our existence. We might even be able to turn the clash of civilizations into a much more productive and even romantic coalition of civilizations, with one foot firmly rooted in a Western, democratic, liberal tradition and the other foot rooted in an Eastern, religious commitment to belief in and obedience toward the word of God.

Notes

1 Yomah, 72b. Midrash Rabba Vayikra, 9:3; 35:6.
2 Genesis, chap. 4.
3 Bereshit Rabba, 22:16.
4 Rita Gillmon, "Noted Theologian Hans Kung to Speak at UCSD, Synagogue," *The San Diego Union*, 9 March 1991, B11.
5 Alaya Keissar-Sugarmen, "A Portrait of Israeli Jews: Beliefs, Observance, and Values of Israeli Jews, 2009," Jerusalem: Israel Democracy Institute, 2009. Available at <http://www.idi.org.il/sites/english/PublicationsCatalog/Pages/Book_7783/Main.aspx>.
6 Job, 25:2.
7 Madeleine Albright, *The Mighty and the Almighty: Reflections on America, God, and World Affairs*, New York: HarperCollins, 2006.
8 Bava Metzi'a, 2a.

Index

Federal Solutions to Ethnic Problems

Accommodating Diversity

By **Liam Anderson**

Series: **Exeter Studies in Ethno Politics**

Exploring five distinct models of federal arrangement, this book evaluates the relative merits of each model as a mechanism for managing relations in ethnically divided societies. Two broad approaches to this issue, accommodation and denial, are identified and, from this, five distinct models of federal arrangement are derived. The models; ethnic, anti-ethnic, territorial, ethno-territorial, and federacy, are defined and then located within their broader theoretical tradition.

Detailed case studies are used to evaluate the strengths and weakness of each model and highlight patterns in the success and failure rates of the universe of post-1945 federal arrangements.

Federal Solutions to Ethnic Problems: Accommodating Diversity advances a new argument within the field of comparative politics, that certain forms of federal arrangement are systematically more successful than others in ameliorating ethnically conflicted societies and is essential reading for students and scholars with an interest in politics and the Middle East.

November 2012: 234x156: 352pp
HB: 978-0-415-78161-9
Eb: 978-0-203-08202-7

Related titles from Routledge

State Reform and Development in the Middle East

Turkey and Egypt in the Post-Liberalization Era

By **Amr Adly**

Series: Routledge Studies in Middle Eastern Economies

The economies of Turkey and Egypt, remarkably similar until the early 1980s, have since taken divergent paths. Turkey has successfully implemented a policy of export led industrialisation whilst Egypt's manufacturing industry and exports have stagnated.

In this book, Amr Adly uses extensive primary research to present detailed comparisons of Turkey's and Egypt's state administrative and private sector capacities and links between the two. The conclusion the author draws is that the external contexts for both were so alike that this cannot account for their diverging paths. Instead, the author suggests a counterintuitive yet compelling explanation; that a democratic polity is far more likely than an authoritarian one to engender a successful developmental state.

Emerging in the wake of the January revolution in Egypt, when hopes for democratisation were raised, this book provides a fresh perspective on the topical subject of state reform and development in the Middle East and will be of interest to students and scholar alike.

November 2012: 234x156: 272pp
Hb: 978-0-415-62419-0
Eb: 978-0-203-10017-2

For more information and to order a copy visit
www.routledge.com/9780415624190/

Available from all good bookshops

The Middle East Today

Political, Geographical and Cultural Perspectives, 2nd Edition

By **Dona Stewart**

The new edition of The Middle East Today provides an accessible and comprehensive introductory textbook for undergraduate students of Middle East Studies, Middle East politics and geography. This updated and revised edition features a host of pedagogical features to assist students with their learning, including; detailed maps and images, case studies on key issues, boxed sections and suggestions for further reading.

The book highlights the current issues facing the Middle East, linking them to the rich political, geographical and cultural history of the region. The author examines the crises and conflicts, both current and potential, likely to dominate the region in coming years.

The second edition has been fully updated and revised to include discussion of such recent events as:
•the effects of the Arab Spring
•Turkey's growing influence in the region
•the dramatic increase in Iran's nuclear capabilities
•Usama bin Laden's death and declining support for violent extremist movements in the Middle East.

Further supplemented by a companion website containing sample chapters, a selection of maps formatted for use in presentations, and annotated links to online resources and websites, The Middle East Today is an essential resource for all students of Middle East Studies, Middle East politics and geography.

November 2012: 234x156: 304pp
Pb: 978-0-415-78244-9
Hb: 978-0-415-78243-2
Eb: 978-0-203-82896-0

For more information and to order a copy visit
www.routledge.com/9780415782449/

Available from all good bookshops